MW00623992

"*The Breakthrough Speaker* is a practical and powerful guide for anyone who wants to build their personal brand and grow their speaking career."
**– Dorie Clark, adjunct professor at Duke University's Fuqua School of Business, contributor to *Harvard Business Review*, author of *Entrepreneurial You***

"Smiley's voice is what every speaker needs to face their fear, get onstage, and give their most authentic performance."
**– Amber Rae, author of *Choose Wonder Over Worry***

"Everybody wins when our networks expand to include a diversity of voices and ideas. Thank you Smiley for sharing your truth and providing a roadmap for others to be heard."
**– J. Kelly Hoey, author of *Build Your Dream Network***

"A playbook for impact-driven makers, storytellers, and leaders."
**– Debbie Sterling, founder and CEO, GoldieBlox**

"Genius book! Smiley's gifts are pure gold for all of those breakthrough speakers waiting in the wings."
**– Claude Silver, chief heart officer, VaynerMedia**

"We need more diversity on stage, and we need more books like this one, which give speakers a toolkit to share their voice with the world."
**– Talia Bender, chief catalyst officer, The Female Quotient**

"Crafting a compelling story is tough, making money while doing it on stage is even harder. Smiley's lessons and constructive encouragement in *The Breakthrough Speaker* are a MUST for anyone, especially women, looking for their own breakthrough on the speaker circuit!"
**– Cassidy Blackwell, director of strategic projects for public affairs, Airbnb**

"Candid, comprehensive, inspiring, and actionable. A no B.S. guide covering all the things nobody ever shares honestly when it comes to corporate speaking."
**– Vanessa Shaw, founder of Human Side of Tech and The Workplace Lab**

"There are so many people whose ideas, messages, and stories should be heard, but who are being held back by lack of access to information or lack of confidence in their value and worth. With this book, Smiley connects the reader not only to everything they'll need to know to launch their speaking career, but also to the conviction that they can succeed."
**– Dr. Emily Anhalt, speaker**

"If you're looking for an inspirational millennial leader, don't look any further. Smiley spoke at SAP's biggest gathering of customers, influencers and business leaders and provided the audience with real insight and better understanding of what young people want from employers today."
**– Robin Meyerhoff, senior director of global corporate affairs, SAP**

"I first saw Smiley speak at Culture Summit, and knew he was the perfect person to speak to the rest of MailChimp about having a career with purpose. The office was buzzing all afternoon after Smiley's Coffee Hour talk. I was thrilled that we brought Smiley in to speak to our employees."
**– Ashley Wilson, employee program and events manager, MailChimp**

"If you want to tap into the mindset of millennials, the person to ask is Adam Smiley Poswolsky."
**– *Forbes***

# THE BREAKTHROUGH SPEAKER

## HOW TO BUILD A PUBLIC SPEAKING CAREER

## SMILEY POSWOLSKY

20s & 30s Press
San Francisco

First edition, 20s & 30s Press, 2018

Portions of this book ("Storyboard your talk," "Write a book that matters," "Prepare for the future of conferences and experience design") have been previously published by the author in Medium and LinkedIn.

20s & 30s Press
Smiley Poswolsky LLC
San Francisco, California

ISBN (paperback): 978-0-9914044-2-1
ISBN (e-book): 978-0-9914044-3-8

Edited by Caroline Kessler
Cover design by Samantha Russo
Book design by Sumeet Banerji
Author photo by Jayson Carpenter

Discounted bulk purchases of this book are available, please contact the author.

www.thebreakthroughspeaker.com
www.smileyposwolsky.com

Printed in the United States of America

*This book was rejected by publishers.*

*They told me it was too niche. They told me there wasn't an audience for it.*

*They told me there weren't enough new voices interested in public speaking.*

*This book is for everyone out there who is proving them wrong.*

*This book is for you.*

# Table of Contents

## Introduction: You belong on stage

## Part I: Speak your truth

## Part II: Share your truth

## Part III: Get paid for your truth

# Introduction:
# You belong on stage

**MY JOURNEY TO BECOMING** a professional public speaker began by accident. If you had told me five years ago that I was going to be making $100,000 a year as a public speaker—that my actual "day job" was going to be flying around the world, all expenses paid, to talk for thirty minutes and tell jokes about struggling to get dates on Tinder and having Facebook-induced FOMO—I would have fallen out of my chair from laughing so hard. I would have spilled kombucha all over myself.

At the time, I was stuck in a job working for the U.S. government that stressed me out so much I got shingles and had panic attacks before falling asleep. Once, I even threw my alarm clock out my window when NPR came on at 6:30 in the morning to wake me up. My job was perfect on paper—I had a good salary, health care, benefits, and job security (trust me, you can't get fired from working for the U.S. government—look who's running the show right now)—but I wasn't personally connected to the work I was doing. I spent hours comparing myself to my friends on Facebook, jealous of how happy they all looked.

In 2012, I left my comfortable job at the U.S. Peace Corps in Washington, D.C, with the intention to not live one more day failing to reach my full potential. I moved 3,000 miles across the country to San Francisco to follow my dream of becoming a writer. When I got here, I began blogging about other millennial social entrepreneurs going after their dreams: people like Debbie Sterling, founder and CEO of GoldieBlox, a toy company that teaches young girls engineering skills; and Ted Gonder, founder of Moneythink, a nonprofit that teaches financial literacy and entrepreneurship to urban high school students; and Tom D'Eri, co-founder and COO of Rising Tide Car Wash, a small business in south Florida that employs people with autism.

In 2013, a friend told me I should write a book about my wandering career journey and the fact that I had eight jobs since graduating college in 2005. I thought he was joking. But, eventually I took him—and myself—seriously. In 2014, I self-published a book about how I turned my quarter-life crisis into a breakthrough. The book featured dozens of stories of other 20- and 30-somethings who were figuring out how to find meaningful work and pay their rent in the midst of an economic recession.

My self-published book launched my speaking career. I didn't even know speaking was something I was good at or that I liked doing. It turned out, public speaking made me feel far more alive than writing did. The first time I ever spoke in front of an audience was the book release party for my self-published book. I spent $100 to rent out Alley Cat Books, a small independent bookstore in the Mission District of San Francisco, and I served cheese and crackers, cheap wine, and PBRs. For the record, my first speaking gig *cost me* about $200. But it was so worth it. I realized that my friends seemed far more engaged with my stories when I was sharing them in person than when I sent them a chapter of the book.

I put together a DIY book tour that included stops pretty much anywhere someone was willing to hear me rant. I would hesitate to call these "gigs." My book tour included speaking on my friend's porch in Washington, D.C., at a hipster beer garden in Brooklyn, and from the *bima* at my parent's synagogue in Cambridge, Massachusetts. The last time I had given a talk inside a synagogue was at my own bar mitzvah, in 1996!

I'd lug around a bag of books with me wherever I went, to San Francisco, New York, Boston, D.C., and London. I'd bust out my intro line, "Raise your hand if you've ever had a quarter-life crisis!" everywhere I traveled, including on the BART, the subway, the Metro, the T, and the Tube. Once, I even sold a book to someone sitting next to me on an airplane during the safety video presentation.

The success of my self-published book on Amazon eventually led to a book deal with Penguin Random House to publish a new version of *The Quarter-Life Breakthrough:*

*Invent Your Own Path, Find Meaningful Work, and Build a Life That Matters* in 2016. The published book led to more speaking opportunities, and slowly the informal speaking gigs at bookstores and hipster bars turned into opportunities to speak at big conferences like TEDx, SAP Sapphire, and Wisdom 2.0, at Fortune 500 companies like Deloitte, Salesforce, Unilever, and Genentech, and at colleges across the country. As a perk, I got to travel around the world (on someone else's dime) to give presentations in places like London, Stockholm, Munich, Lisbon, Vienna, and Dubrovnik.

I learned a few important lessons early on in my speaking career:

1.  **Do not wait for permission.** No one ever told me I could be an author or that I was a professional speaker. I just started doing it. If you wait until Chris Anderson invites you to give a TED talk (and believe me, I check my inbox every day just hoping to see an email from that dude), you're never going to become a professional speaker. If you wait until a speaker agent invites you to sign with them, you're never going to become a speaker either. The only person who can give you permission is yourself.

2.  **Start now.** If you want to be a speaker, start speaking today. The venue can be your friend's office, your local coffee shop, even your living room. Get a few

people together and share your truth. I recently spoke at ATECH, a tech conference in Aruba focused on building the start-up ecosystem in the Caribbean. The governor of Aruba was in the front row. I used a joke during my talk that I first shared back on my friend's front porch in Washington, D.C., three years ago. Guess what? The governor was laughing out loud. You don't need a fancy stage or an invitation from a big tech conference. You just need a story and a few people to listen.

3. **Call yourself a speaker.** People will not book you or pay you for something you do not have confidence to call yourself. Put the word 'SPEAKER' on your website, LinkedIn, and business card. Tell everyone you know they should book you to speak.

4. **You belong on stage.** When I first started going to conferences to speak, I was very nervous. I had imposter syndrome and felt like I didn't belong. It seemed like the other speakers were part of some secret nightclub and I was a loser that had somehow snuck past the bouncer. As I started watching other speakers' presentations, I became less and less intimidated. Sure, a few speakers were really good. Some of them were definitely better than me. But they weren't *that* much better, and most speakers out there were pretty damn awful. I thought, "I can do

this. I got this. I belong on stage too." Don't put your impossible dreams of becoming a paid speaker on hold. Speakers are humans too and not necessarily any different from you, other than the fact that one day, they just started practicing.

5. **Your story matters.** Often, we assume that the only people who deserve to speak are famous, powerful, or successful. Early on, I realized, "Holy shit, I have something to say. People want to hear my story. People need to hear my story." The truth is that someone out there is waiting to hear your story and you're the only person who can tell it.

6. **This stuff takes time.** This is important: *it took me four years total to make any significant money from public speaking*. It took two years from the time I quit my job until the time my self-published book came out, and another two years for the Penguin-published version of the book to come out. I did nearly fifty unpaid speaking engagements in 2014 and 2015 before booking my first paid speaking gig. Making income from speaking takes time, but if you're willing to practice and be patient, there is a tremendous opportunity for both income and impact.

7. **Speaking is far more lucrative than writing.** When I moved to San Francisco, I wanted to be a writer. I love

to write and writing will always be part of my life. But the truth is, if I had to rely solely on writing to make a living, I'd have been forced to get a real job years ago. Beyond a book deal, authors usually make very little money on their books. But, writing a book opens up lucrative opportunities for speaking, teaching, consulting, coaching, and other business opportunities. To be transparent, I was paid about $50,000 for the published version of my book, which took about four years in total to produce. That breaks down to about $12,500 a year, before the agent's cut and taxes. In contrast, I've made over $200,000 from my speaking business in the past two years. I receive opportunities for well-paid speaking gigs every week. Until you're a *New York Times* bestselling author, your real revenue is not going to come from writing—it's going to come from speaking.

8. **You are undercharging for your work.** Not long after I started public speaking, I realized I was consistently undervaluing my work and not asking for enough money. Once you've practiced, and then practiced some more, you'll have the confidence to stand in your worth. Figure out what your peers with similar experience in your field are charging and make the bold, fearless ask for money. Your fee is a reflection of your power. Clients will respect you more if you believe in what you are worth.

9. **The speaking industry is old, white, male, and boring. There has never been a better time to break in and shake up this archaic industry.** When I started speaking at conferences, I realized that the speaking circuit was just that: a never-ending rotation of Boring Old White Dudes (BOWDs). Their suits were worn down. Their PowerPoints were full of ClipArt and illegible charts in ten-point font that you couldn't even read from the first row, with way too many bullet points. Their anecdotes felt dated and irrelevant. Their content was dull. Their jokes were corny. It looked like they hadn't been excited about giving a talk since 1992. These guys were phoning it in, and so were most of the conference organizers booking them.

For too long the corporate speaking world has been a secret old white boys club where people seem to sneak their way in and then lock the gates behind them as quickly as possible. Too many BOWDs in ill-fitting khakis have realized it's a lucrative field ("Wow, I can get paid $15,000 an hour to give the same talk I've given since Bill Clinton was president? This is amazing!") and they haven't told anyone, certainly not anyone that doesn't look like them, how they did it. The speaking circuit is too old, too male, too white, too straight, and too boring. The intention of this book is to change that.

## Why this book?

The public speaking industry is booming around the world. In 2016, in the U.S. alone, the meetings industry, the backbone of the speaking circuit, generated $325 billion in direct spending and $845 billion in business sales. In 2016, 1.6 million meetings were held in the U.S, welcoming more than 250 million attendees. There are five TEDx events organized every day in 130 countries. Every day, 1.5 million TED talks are watched online. These videos are translated into 90 different languages. More and more people watch the news, share their ideas, and communicate via online video. *Every single minute*, 300 hours of video are uploaded on YouTube, 400 hours of new video are shared, and seven million videos are watched on Snapchat.

Public speaking has become an essential life skill. In previous decades, the barometer for successful thought leadership was publishing a book. Today, it's delivering a TED talk. With the growing popularity of YouTube, Instagram stories, Facebook video, and Snapchat, especially among millennials and Gen-Z, public speaking has become a crucial and lucrative way for people to promote their personal brand and generate income. Every millennial I meet asks me, "How did you break into the speaking industry? How did you start getting paid to speak?"

In addition to becoming more popular, the speaking industry is changing quickly. The speaker circuit is becoming more diverse, younger, more interactive, and more experiential. Event participants around the world (and their followers on Twitter) are finally demanding new voices on stage. Op-eds have exposed the antiquated speaking circuit for what it is: a never-ending parade of white men. A recent article in *The Atlantic* cited research proving that women are invited to give fewer talks than men at top U.S. universities. *Forbes* did an exposé on the pay gap between men and women speakers at tech conferences. *Mic* ran a popular article titled, "Think there aren't qualified women in tech? Here are 1,000 names. No more excuses." The blog, "Congrats: you have an all-male panel!" went viral.

When I think of an effective public speaker, I don't think of a boring old white dude with gray hair sharing yet another story about Steve Jobs and leadership; I think of Emma Gonzalez, an 18 year-old high school student who had just experienced the trauma of watching her best friends and classmates killed by a school shooter in Parkland, Florida, passionately calling attention to the total bullshit that is our country's gun control problem, declaring on national television,

**"If the President wants to come up to me and tell me to my face that it was a terrible tragedy and that it should never have happened and maintain telling us that nothing is going to be done about it, I'm gonna happily ask him how much money he received from the National Rifle Association. But hey, you want to**

know something, it doesn't matter, because I already know. $30 million dollars! And divided by the number of gunshot victims in the United States in the one and one-half months in 2018 alone, that comes out to being $5800. Is that how much these people are worth to you, Trump?… To every politician that is taking donations from the NRA, shame on you!"

Emma's speech was viewed more than three million times on YouTube, and her voice, and the voices of her classmates and other young leaders around the country—many of them young women of color—have sparked a new youth-led movement for gun control in America. As Emma's words teach us, it's time to start speaking up about the issues that matter most.

Change happens when someone is brave enough to speak out.

It's time for the public speaking industry to make space for passionate young voices like Emma's. It's time to call BS on any event that doesn't commit to inclusive representation on stage. I'm tired of going to conferences and companies and finding that the only speakers on stage look like me. I'm interested in helping any speaker who has a story to share, but I'm particularly interested in empowering voices that haven't yet had the chance to be heard, and giving event planners and those in positions of power the resources to find new voices. I think it's important for men, specifically white men, to champion these causes, especially in an industry that is often controlled by them.

Together, we can break the floodgates wide open and revolutionize who we see—and who we pay—to speak. If we don't ensure an equal representation of speakers on stage, can we really be surprised that only one in five C-Suite leaders is a woman, that just one in thirty is a woman of color, that there are currently only four black CEOs in the Fortune 500, and zero, yes *zero*, black women running Fortune 500 companies?

If we don't compensate our speakers, authors, influencers, and leaders fairly, then how can we expect to have true equity, inclusion, and belonging in the spaces we write and speak about? If we don't compensate our speakers fairly, then can we really be surprised that white non-Hispanic women are paid 81 cents on the dollar compared to white non-Hispanic men, that Asian women are paid 88 cents on the dollar, and that black and Hispanic women are paid just 65 cents and 59 cents on the white male dollar, respectively?

If you're also interested in championing women and people of color speakers, please join The Women Speaker Initiative, a network and community of more than a thousand people, which aims to increase the number of women and people of color speaking at conferences and companies, and ensure that women and POC speakers are paid competitively. Check out the Resources in the back of this book, which includes lists of brilliant women and POC speakers to invite when organizing your next event. 100 percent of the profits from sales of this book will go to support efforts of The Women Speaker Initiative, so by reading, you've already made a commitment to ensure more diverse voices are represented on stage all over the world.

## Who is this book for?

This is the book I wish I had when I first realized public speaking might be something I could actually make money doing. I didn't know who to turn to with my questions about the speaking industry because I didn't have a single friend who actually got paid to speak. There wasn't a great resource to read about how to ask for money, what to charge, and how to leverage speaking at conferences into paid engagements. All of the $997.97 online trainings and webinars about public speaking felt sleazy, salesy, and poorly done—and most of them had been made by BOWDs.

This book started as answers to questions I was getting about public speaking. The goal of this practical guide is to help you share your message to the world, and earn good money while you do it. Most books about speaking focus on the mechanics of storytelling, how to deliver a compelling narrative or pitch, and the art of public speaking. Without mastering these communications skills, people will not be interested in what you have to say.

Billionaire investor Warren Buffet once said that you can improve your career value by 50 percent simply by learning public speaking skills. I highly recommend you read Chris Anderson's book *TED Talks*, and Carmine Gallo's *Talk Like TED* before reading this guide. These books will help you construct a narrative people remember and make you a better orator.

However, few books actually break down step-by-step how you can build a profitable speaking business in 2018 and beyond. Giving an unpaid TEDx talk at a small university is cool; but getting paid thousands of dollars an hour to give a corporate talk is *really cool*. So, how do you actually make money from public speaking? How do you turn your fifteen-minute TEDx talk or thirty-minute keynote or ninety-minute workshop into a business that can generate anywhere from $2,000 to $20,000 per hour? How do you break into an archaic corporate speaking industry that is dominated by BOWDs?

This book will you help you get paid for your story. Being a keynote speaker is the Holy Grail of thought leadership. It's one of the most well-respected and well-compensated professions in business. I've titled this book *The Breakthrough Speaker* because I think it's possible for a hard-working speaker to break through and get paid thousands of dollars an hour for their speaking practice. You don't need to be famous or have a giant social media following to make $50,000 or even $100,000 a year from speaking.

The reason I make money from speaking is not

because I'm famous, because I'm not famous at all—although my local avocado toast shop does know my order by heart. The reason I make money from speaking is because I've worked really hard at it for a long time, and because I speak about something audiences care about. It's really that simple (and impossible), which is why this book exists.

My mission in life is to help people find meaningful work, and there is nothing more meaningful than standing up in front of a room and sharing your story. I can't tell you how wonderful it is to receive emails from people who tell me they watched my TEDx talk and were inspired to quit an oppressive job, start a new career, launch a blog, write a book, start their own business, move to a new city, and find purpose in their life. If you're spending your life sharing your story, chances are your life will be filled with meaning. You'll spend your days helping people and organizations, which is truly fulfilling. You'll gain the financial flexibility and the career autonomy to pursue projects you care deeply about. You'll get job offers when you're not even looking for a job. You'll have the opportunity to travel the world (for free), and meet influential and inspiring people everywhere you go. You'll build the personal brand you need to survive and succeed in today's unstable and unpredictable job market.

The lessons in this book will help new speakers break into the corporate speaking industry, as well as entrepreneurs, creatives, and influencers who want to gain exposure and make a greater impact. Whether you want to become a full-time professional speaker, speak a few times a year as a side hustle to supplement your income, or speak on panels to share the good work your organization is doing, the lessons in this book will help you get discovered, build your platform, raise your career capital, and become a respected leader within your field.

## What is a Breakthrough Speaker?

In short, this book is for people who want to become Breakthrough Speakers. What is a Breakthrough Speaker? It means that whether you speak several times a year, or speak several times a week, *you want to speak your truth, share your truth, and get paid for your truth. It means you want to do the deep and challenging work necessary to grow your public speaking business and make your mark on the world.* Let's break down the key differences between Wannabee Speakers and Breakthrough Speakers.

1.  Wannabee Speakers tell audiences to follow their passion and quit their job.
    **Passion is fluff. Passion is fleeting. Passion is played out. Passion is something unemployed life coaches in Bali talk about. Breakthrough Speakers know that passion will not get you paid. Breakthrough Speakers know that companies don't pay speakers to tell their**

**employees to quit their job—they pay speakers to make their employees do a better job. Breakthrough Speakers know that expertise in a subject that people care about will get you paid.**

2. Wannabee speakers tell audiences how much they've accomplished. Wannabee speakers talk about their start-up.
   **There is nothing more boring than a speaker who goes on and on about their professional accomplishments. If you're on stage, people already know you're cool—you don't need to prove it. Breakthrough Speakers share a story that connects, educates, inspires, and endures. Breakthrough Speakers share a story that matters.**

3. Wannabee speakers have three or four talks they try to sell. Wannabee speakers think they are qualified to speak about seven different topics. Wannabee speakers speak about vague and broad topics like "innovation," "leadership," "motivation," and "productivity."
   **Breakthrough Speakers are focused. Breakthrough Speakers carve a highly-specific niche, and then a niche within their niche. Breakthrough Speakers spend a year or two (or more!) mastering one keynote, before adding another talk to their business. Breakthrough Speakers know that becoming a one-hit wonder is the best way to launch their speaking**

**career.**

4.  Wannabee speakers think they can be booked to speak on the merits of their stage presence alone.
    **Breakthrough Speakers craft an anchor that matters (like a book, product, creative endeavor, influential job, social movement) to grow their speaking business.**

5.  Wannabee speakers just want to make money.
    **Breakthrough Speakers want to get paid, but they share their truth in a way that empowers their audience. Wannabee speakers are out for themselves and their bank accounts, while Breakthrough Speakers are driven by a higher purpose. Breakthrough Speakers want to build a movement and make an impact.**

6.  Wannabee speakers speak for free.
    **Breakthrough Speakers know that there is no such thing as speaking for free. Even if they are speaking for no money, Breakthrough Speakers still ask for invaluable assets like video, media, testimonials, and referrals which will help them book paid gigs in the future.**

7.  Wannabee speakers don't negotiate their speaking fee.
    **Breakthrough Speakers always negotiate their speaking fee. Breakthrough Speakers always ask for**

more money. Breakthrough Speakers stand in their worth.

8. Wannabee speakers spend the majority of their time posting on Instagram about how cool they are.
   **Breakthrough Speakers know that social media alone will not get them speaking gigs, and that their website is far more important than their Instagram feed. Breakthrough Speakers work hard to create an echo chamber across multiple mediums on the Internet, to make sure they are demonstrating their subject matter expertise. Breakthrough Speakers know that social media is only a tiny part of the puzzle.**

9. Wannabee speakers think they are rock stars.
   **Breakthrough Speakers know that the surest way to piss off a client (and the audience) is to act like a diva. Breakthrough Speakers treat everyone they meet at a gig (from the person booking them to the A/V team to the catering staff) with respect. Breakthrough Speakers know that it's not about them, it's about everyone else in the room. Breakthrough Speakers approach their craft from a place of service, not stardom.**

10. Wannabee speakers nominate themselves to speak at every single event in the world.
    **Breakthrough Speakers know there are certain**

events they are a good fit for, based on their topic expertise and experience, and other events that are not a good fit. If they come across an event that's not a good fit, they nominate someone else they know who would be a better fit. Breakthrough Speakers know they don't walk alone. Breakthrough Speakers are committed to increasing diversity, representation, and opportunity in public speaking.

## How to use this book

This book shares lessons I've learned in my journey from an unpaid storyteller to a paid speaker who is regularly paid $10,000 for 30-minute presentations. **Part I: Speak your truth** will help you discover your story, craft an anchor to earn credibility, and discover how to align your zone of genius with a top-of-mind hook that organizations care about and are willing to invest in. **Part II: Share your truth** will give you the marketing tools to spread your message, reach a wider audience, and make your work stand out from the crowd. **Part III: Get paid for your truth** provides tips for you to break into the corporate speaking industry, stand in your worth, negotiate higher speaking fees, and become a speaker who clients love.

Like any craft, public speaking takes years of practice, so I recommend setting aside time and space to go deeper and do the exercises in each section. Having said that, every speaker is unique and coming to this book with different levels of experience and personal goals. If some of the exercises don't work for you, skip them. If some sections don't apply to you, or feel too elementary given your background, feel free to jump around to the sections that are calling to you. Make this guide work for you.

In addition to sharing my journey, I've included the stories, experiences, and anecdotes of other speakers I know. Like me, these speakers are not famous—or at least not yet. They're hustlers building their paid speaking career from scratch, just like you, just like me. Some of them have just booked their first paid gig, some of them make well over $100,000 a year from public speaking. Some of them are on the other side of the coin, selecting speakers for prestigious events like TED, international conferences, and major speaking agencies. If you want more helpful content and interviews, check out *smileyposwolsky.com/ thebreakthroughspeaker*.

If you're reading this, chances are the stage is calling your name for a reason, and your breakthrough speaking career has already begun. Let's do this.

# PART I.
# SPEAK
# YOUR TRUTH

# 1

# Why we speak

**MY FAVORITE QUESTION** to ask a public speaker is why they started speaking. But you have to be careful. Asking this question is like starting Season 1 of *Game of Thrones*—once you dive in, you better not have anywhere to be for a while. Every speaker has a unique origin story, but we all share a common bond that at some point, something in our lives got us so annoyed, so furious, so enthralled, so enchanted, so riled up that we said, *"To hell with it, I'm going to stand up, start talking, and people are going to listen to me."*

I started speaking because I was in pain. Not just existential pain, but physical pain. Being stuck in a job that was perfect in my parents' eyes, but made me miserable, and having no idea how to quit or what I wanted to do with my life gave me immense anxiety. I had shingles, panic attacks, and night sweats. I was experiencing a quarter-life crisis, and I felt lost and alone.

Furthermore, I felt like my generation was deeply misunderstood. I saw all these memes about millennials being lazy and entitled, the "me, me, me" generation, and I was like, "Entitled?! Motherfucker, I'm almost 30 years old, and I still have thousands of dollars in student loans to pay off! Sallie Mae: if I ever see you on Tinder, I'm swiping left. All my friends are broke and working their asses off to pay their bills. Some of them have two or three jobs. We're not lazy or entitled, we're looking for something more than just a job and a paycheck—we're looking for purpose." So began my captivation (and my speaking career) with millennials, meaningful work, and the changing nature of the modern workplace.

When I interviewed my friend Minda Harts, founder of The Memo LLC, a career development company for women of color, she told me she started speaking because of lack of representation. She was tired of going to events and panels and not seeing anyone that looked like her on stage. "It wasn't something I always knew I wanted to do, I more so started out of *if not me, then who*?" Minda explains. "And the more I began to tell my story, the more women started contacting me and my speaking engagements increased. Women, but especially women of color want to see themselves in the speakers. It feels good to see yourself and careers are a good place to start."

I recently shared the stage with Robin Farmanfar-maian at a tech conference in Munich. She was speaking about healthcare because of her own miserable experience with the healthcare system. When she was just a teen-ager, Robin was misdiagnosed by her doctors, resulting in forty-three hospitalizations, six major surgeries, and three lost organs. As she explains in one of her talks, "No doctors ever looked at me and said, 'Let's hold off on these surgeries because you're so young and technology is moving so quickly,' nobody ever looked at me and said, technology is hope." Robin is the author of *The Patient as CEO* and *The Thought Leader Formula*, and she has spoken over 125 times in 12 countries about the future of technology in medicine.

One of my favorite speakers, Ashanti Branch, told me he had wanted to be a motivational speaker ever since he was young, when someone handed him a tape of Les Brown, and he listened to it several hundred times. Ashanti was raised by a single mother on welfare in Oakland, California, and went on to study civil engineering at California Polytechnic State University, San Luis Obispo. It wasn't until years later when Ashanti left engineering to become a high school teacher in San Lorenzo, California, that he discovered he was becoming a motivational speaker simply from having to motivate his students every day. "As a teacher I realized that a lot of my work was motivating my students to do their work, and a lot less of it was how much I could teach them," Ashanti says. "Many of them were super smart, but they did not always come to school with a focus on learning, so I wanted to inspire them to believe in themselves more. There's very little in the curriculum that allows you to help motivate students, you have to put that into the curriculum and that became my mission every day; to always give inspiring words and let [my students] know that their work could take them to amazing places if they just sacrificed some time and energy to do it."

Today, Ashanti is the founder and executive director of the Ever Forward Club, which creates a safe space for underserved and at-risk young men of color to talk about what's going on in their lives without worry of feeling ashamed. The Ever Forward Club has helped 100 percent of its members graduate high school, and 93 percent of them have gone on to attend college, trade schools or the military. Ashanti has spoken about vulnerability, mental health, and masculinity at schools and conferences around the world, in places like Australia, Mexico, Bermuda, and Colombia. In 2015, his work was featured in Jennifer Siebel Newsom's Netflix documentary *The Mask You Live In*, about boys and young men struggling to find themselves within America's narrow definition of masculinity.

Minda, Robin, Ashanti, and I all had something we wanted to prove and something we wanted to get off our chest, even though the specifics of our journeys are different. We each had an audience that we were (and still are) committed to serving. *Why did you start speaking? What do you need to get off your chest? How do you feel unseen or misunderstood? What problem are you trying to solve? Who do you want to serve?*

# Exercise: Call your friend

The first exercise is for people who want to do more public speaking but don't know where to start. Call a few people that know you well, like a sibling, partner, best friend, or family member. Even better, you could hang out with them in person. Ask them: *what do they think you should speak about? What are the stories you always tell that are most interesting? What can't you stop talking about? What are you trying to get off your chest?* For example, if I had done this exercise with my grandmother back in the day when she was still with us, I would have been like, "Grandma! You need to speak about food. All you ever do is talk about food—we're not even done with lunch yet, and you're talking about dinner. At dinner, you're talking about what we should have for lunch tomorrow!" Chances are, the people in your life that love you most know what you should speak about, since they've been listening to your rants and stories forever.

# 2

# What's your story?

**THERE'S ONLY ONE PLACE** to begin a book about speaking your truth and it's with why you're here. The best speakers don't speak, they tell stories. Stories that connect, educate, inspire, endure, and leave the audience forever changed. If you have a good story—and everyone has a good story, you can change the way people see themselves and the world.

In *The Faraway Nearby*, Rebecca Solnit writes, "What's your story? It's all in the telling. Stories are compasses and architecture; we navigate by them, we build our sanctuaries and our prisons out of them, and to be without a story is to be lost in the vastness of a world that spreads in all directions like artic tundra or sea ice." So, what's your internal compass? Your personal architecture? The soil or foundation on which you live your life? How do you show up every day? What makes you *you*? What narratives, experiences, history, family, characters, knowledge, and dreams do you bring with you when you go out into the world? Why did you start reading this book?

You can't make this shit up. Elle Luna and Susie Herrick write in their beautiful book, *Your Story Is Your*

*Power: Free Your Feminine Voice*, "In the heart of your story, you will find *you*, your voice, your power, and your truth." As I started building my speaking career, I quickly learned there were two types of speakers: the type who tried to be someone they weren't, and the type who was authentically and fully in their body and their narrative. Your goal is to be yourself and share something you are uniquely capable of sharing. There is nothing worse than seeing an introvert get on stage and try to be a hype person. If you're not the emcee for an event, if your name isn't Flavor Flav, it's not your job to get people pumped up. If you're not a meditation teacher, please don't lead a group meditation. If you're not funny, don't try to be Dave Chappelle. If you work for a large oil and gas corporation, don't get up there and start quoting Martin Luther King Jr. If you run a five-person startup that's looking for funding, don't quote Steve Jobs. As Chris Anderson writes in *TED Talks*, "Your goal is not to be Winston Churchill or Nelson Mandela. It's to be you."

Building a strong keynote presentation starts with having a really strong message that you can summarize in just a few minutes with a central story, a key idea, and a few pieces of evidence or anecdotes to back up your argument. So, reflect on your own story. *Who are you? What do you love about yourself? What do you love about the world? What makes you sad? What is your most sacred memory of a loved one? What do you really care about? How do you spend your time? What have you learned in your life? Who taught you these lessons? What social injustice makes you get out of bed in the morning? If you only had several minutes to share your truth with the world, what would that truth be?*

## Exercise: Moments that matter

Take out your journal or a notebook. Reflect on the most important moments that have shaped your life. If you're stuck, pick one memorable moment from childhood, one from high school or college, and one from your life after graduation. Some examples to get you started might be: a turning point in your career, the death of a family member or close friend, going away to college, getting your first job, starting your first business, getting fired, moving to a new city, living abroad, falling in love, getting your heart broken. Write down as much as you can about these moments. What happened? Who else was there? What did you lose? What did you find? What did you learn from these experiences? How did the moment change your life? Now, reflect on the relationship between these moments and where you are today. Is there a connection? If so, describe it.

# 3

# Fear is a good sign

IF YOU'RE AFRAID OF PUBLIC SPEAKING, you're not alone. Surveys show that people rank their fear of getting in front of a group and talking more than they fear death. As comedian Jerry Seinfeld once observed, we'd rather be dead in the coffin than alive and giving the eulogy at a funeral.

I want to share a short story about my friend and freelance writer Hana Nobel, a story that will help anyone who's letting stage fright get in the way of their public speaking career. Hana has always been a big public radio nerd. She loves NPR and in college, she became a fan of the live storytelling show, The Moth. It was something her and her dad shared, and when she graduated from college, they went together to Moth events in Philadelphia.

"I hate public speaking," Hana told me. "I start shaking. It's an anxiety ridden experience from the moment I find out I have to do it, until I do it. Once I get on stage, it's fine. I just black out and I don't remember what happens when I get on stage. So, I don't pursue public speaking. When I do it, it's usually because I'm forced into it."

My guess is that a lot of people feel the way Hana does about public speaking. They only do it when someone else makes them. For Hana's birthday this year, six friends took her to The Moth's StorySLAM in Los Angeles because they knew she loved the event. One friend demanded that she put her name in the hat to perform. (At The Moth, they call ten audience members to perform, one by one, so you don't know whether or not you're going to be called on until the very end of the event.)

"I was praying I didn't get called," Hana said. "Number 9 was called and it wasn't me, so I figured I could get drunk and have a beer. The last name to be read was number 10, and I could hear the host call my name out, 'Hana Nobel!' I was like, 'Motherfucker!'"

Hana went up to the mic and told a funny story about how she got caught attacking the Easter bunny in first grade. She grew up Jewish and her parents had given her intelligence on the Easter bunny and how to prove to her friends it wasn't real. "I blacked out up there," Hana recalls. "I do remember that I told a joke about being a long-time lurker, first-time attacker, and the NPR geeks loved it."

Hana booked it off stage as soon as she was done with her five-minute story and before the judges had even announced their scores. But Hana received a 9.3, 9.5, and 9.7. She won the StorySLAM on her birthday! The only problem was that her prize wasn't a beautiful tote bag as she had been hoping; it was that she has to go on stage at another, larger Moth event at an even bigger theater in LA, and compete against the winners of the other StorySLAMs.

As you can imagine, Hana already had anxiety about the next StorySLAM competition, but she admitted that she's better at public speaking than she first thought. "I'm taking improv classes to feel more comfortable speaking, and I guess I'm okay at it. Or good enough to keep doing it. Strangers were judging me—and they thought I was good at something that I have low confidence in. Maybe I should listen more to other people that notice abilities in myself that I don't notice yet."

I find Hana's story inspiring because it reminds me that sometimes all it takes is a stranger to push us in the direction of our fears. If people have been telling you that you're a good speaker, or that you have a powerful voice, or that you should start sharing your story more often, it's up to you to listen. You just might win one of the most prestigious storytelling events in the country.

## Exercise: Finding your voice

Hana's story teaches us that public speaking isn't about speaking at a business conference. Public speaking is about becoming comfortable with sharing your unique voice with the world. There are a lot of activities you can do to find your voice that have absolutely nothing to do with the corporate speaking industry. In this exercise, you'll pick two new activities to try in the next month that will get you more comfortable being vulnerable with strangers and performing on stage. Most cities have these classes and activities available, and if you're struggling to find them, try searching on Meetup.com.

Here are a few suggested activities to choose from: improv, stand-up comedy, storytelling (like The Moth!), chorus or singing classes, voice lessons, open mic nights, karaoke, authentic connection games, non-violent communication classes, or Dungeons & Dragons (or another group game night). As my friend Erika Barraza, a virtual reality expert who speaks about VR and emerging technologies, once told me, "Finding your voice means being more intentional about your language." So, how can you practice becoming more intentional about what you say? How can you become comfortable with your own weird, wild, and wonderful voice?

# 4

# Move beyond passion

**EVERY SINGLE COURSE** about public speaking begins and ends by telling you to find your passion. "Find your passion, speak about what you're passionate about, and the rest will follow." If only it were so simple. If you want to start speaking, speaking about what you're passionate about is a great place to start. Obviously, you can't speak about something you find boring, and all good speakers are passionate about something. But here's the harsh reality. Passion might get you on stage, but it will not get you paid.

If you want to speak, sure—speak about whatever you want. But if you want to get paid to speak, you have to speak about something that matters, and something that *other people* are passionate about. You need to speak about something that *other people* (specifically people that are in a position to book you to speak) are obsessed with. This is the single most important lesson to keep in mind when building a paid speaking business.

Find the alignment between what other people care about and your own passion. Many an unemployed life coach have tried speaking about whatever they wanted. I've seen it all. Keynotes about hot yoga, kombucha, your invisible inner-power, why you should quit your job and move to Bali, the gift of soaked chia seeds. Blah, blah, blah. If your speaking topic sounds anything like these, my honest advice is to instead find something that people who actually work for a living want to hear. There are hundreds of sales-y online public speaking courses for $997.97 that will lie to you and say you can make thousands of dollars talking about whatever you want. Trust me, you can't.

Instead, you want to be the person talking about a highly relevant topic. People get paid to speak because they are *sharing the right idea by the right person at the right time.* Here are a few questions to think about as you take your personal story and figure out how it fits into the larger, public narrative. *Is your topic specific? Do you (actually) want to speak about your topic? Are you qualified to speak about your topic? Do people want to hear you speak about that topic? Do people (other than unemployed life coaches in Bali) care about your topic? Do people (other than your friends) care about your topic? Does your topic have an industry behind it? Do conferences exist solely about your topic? Is now the right time for someone to be speaking about your topic?*

# 5

# Storyboard your talk

**ONE EXERCISE I USE FOR BOTH** book writing and writing my presentations is storyboarding. In my favorite book about writing, *Bird by Bird*, Anne Lamott talks about the power of short assignments. Whenever you're stuck, you can start with a short prompt that gets you writing a paragraph or two. After a few paragraphs, you're golden. This is how I approach my talks as well.

I start by taking a large stack of Post-it notes and on each Post-it, I write one short story that I want to tell. It could be an anecdote, a quote, a person's name, a joke, an example, a case study, a practical takeaway for employees, or the main idea of the presentation. I don't worry if the stories are in chronological order or even if the stories will end up making the final talk, I simply jot down all the stories I think I want to speak about.

Then, I take the Post-its and spread them over a huge wall. Once they are all spread out, I begin to group them by theme or topic. Some Post-its don't really fit into a particular theme, and that's fine, I leave those to the side. But usually, the Post-its are placed in four or five 'categories', which become the foundation for the four or five parts of my talk. When I'm ready, I go Post-it by Post-it and outline notes for each part of the talk, until it all comes together and I can take away what isn't working and add what's missing.

If you're having trouble thinking of sticky notes, here are a few questions: *What is the single most important idea of your talk? What's a personal story you can tell that illustrates the main idea of your talk? How do the crucible moments you came up with in the previous exercise relate to your current work? What are three examples or anecdotes you can give to support your message? Who is your target audience? What is the feeling you want your audience to have or action you want them to take after your talk?*

## Exercise: Visioning your story

After you've spent time reflecting on your story and the moments that have shaped your life, close your eyes. Take a few deep breaths. Picture yourself on the stage that matters more to you than any other. Maybe you're delivering the State of the Union. Maybe you're at NASA, about to take off to Mars. Maybe you're opening Saturday Night Live. Maybe you're accepting the Nobel Peace Prize or the Pulitzer. Maybe you're quitting your job in front of all your colleagues. Maybe you're giving a toast at your own wedding. *Whatever that stage is, what it is like to be there? How do you feel? What do you say to the audience? What will the audience be inspired to do once you've shared your story?*

You want to channel this energy into writing your story, and then practice it as many times as possible. When I do this exercise, I usually picture myself giving an acceptance speech at the Oscars, which is kind of funny since I don't even work in the film business. So, I spend two minutes picturing myself speaking the at Oscars—everyone there is crying: my mom, Meryl Streep, Chris Rock. Then, I come back to reality and I practice my talk in front of the mirror in my bedroom. Yes, it's kind of silly going from seeing George Clooney and Emma Watson in the front row to being in my bedroom with my dirty underwear lying around, but such is life. Channel that Oscars-level energy as you practice your story.

# 6

# Connect, educate, inspire, endure

**THINK OF THE BEST TALK** you've ever seen. For me, it's definitely Bryan Stevenson's TED talk, "We need to talk about an injustice." Stevenson tells harsh truths about the criminal justice system in America: there are 2.3 million people in U.S. jails and prisons, the highest rate of incarceration in the world, with one out of three black men between the ages of 18 and 30 in jail, in prison, on probation or parole. He shares that in urban communities across the country, like Los Angeles, Philadelphia, Baltimore, and D.C., 50 to 60 percent of all young men of color are in jail, in prison, or on probation or parole.

He delivers this deeply troubling information in a way that is personal, touching, and even funny at times. He talks about his grandmother, his personal identity, Rosa Parks, and why he works as a lawyer defending children from being tried as adults. He closes with a beautiful anecdote about befriending an older black janitor who works at the courthouse where he's defending a client on a challenging case. At some point, the janitor comes into the courtroom and approaches the bench. In Bryan Stevenson's words:

"**And this deputy jumped up and he ran over to this older black man. He said, "Jimmy, what are you doing in this courtroom?" And this older black man stood up and he looked at that deputy and he looked at me and he said, "I came into this courtroom to tell this young man, keep your eyes on the prize, hold on."**

**I've come to TED because I believe that many of you understand that the moral arc of the universe is long, but it bends toward justice. That we cannot be full evolved human beings until we care about human rights and basic dignity. That all of our survival is tied to the survival of everyone. That our visions of technology and design and entertainment and creativity have to be married with visions of humanity, compassion and justice. And more than anything, for those of you who share that, I've simply come to tell you to keep your eyes on the prize, hold on."**

His talk connects, educates, inspires, and endures. I've watched it seven times and I've cried every single time. The best talks—the best stories—provide both inspiration and information. They are told in a way that connects on a deeply personal level, educates the audience about something that matters in the world, and inspires the viewer to go forward and take action or change the way they think, love, work, or live. In fact, after Stevenson's talk, the TED community ended up donating $1.3 million to his organization, the Equal Justice Initiative, which works to end excessive sentencing of children and keep children from being put in adult prisons. If you've seen Stevenson's talk, you know that he never once makes a pitch for money in the actual talk. In fact, Stevenson almost never even went to TED, because he had two Supreme Court cases to argue the same month as the conference.

As you write and practice your talk, think about your balance of substance and style, content and connection, head and heart. The more personal and authentic your anecdotes are, the better. Dawn J. Fraser, an internationally known communications coach and storyteller who has spoken at TED@NYC and worked as a storytelling coach with The Moth, recently told me, "Storytelling, when done well, has the ability to create that connection, and to recognize shared values better than any other form of communication...It's much more interesting to hear about how something has changed someone's life, mind, or perspective, however slight that may be, then to just hear about what the product or service does."

If you spend too much time on content, delivering bullet point after bullet point of statistics, case studies, and information, the audience will quickly fall asleep. But if you don't have substance to add to your powerful stage presence and personal narrative, you won't make it very far in the speaking industry. I find that new speakers tend to lean too far in the direction of style without substance. Their talks feel like unemployed life coaches in Bali giving a sermon about how to live your best life—in other words, aspiration and inspiration, with nothing to back up the fluff. If you're the expert being invited to speak, the audience expects you to be an expert. Practical content (statistics, case studies, research, action items) matters, especially in the corporate speaking industry. Can you tell touching personal stories that *also* use data to move the audience to change their behavior?

## Exercise: Say the things that must be said

One thing that all Breakthrough Speakers have in common is that they are talking about things that few people have the courage to talk about. They are sharing harsh truths that we need to hear, but that are sometimes difficult to talk about. Bryan Stevenson's talk is powerful because he is at TED—a bastion of innovation in technology, education, design—discussing the complete opposite of progress: the horrific and racist American prison industrial complex. As you build your keynote, ask yourself this question: are you sharing something that's difficult for you to talk about? Are you talking about something that might be challenging for the audience to hear? Are you speaking truth to power? Are you saying the things that need to be said? Make a list of all the things in your talk that you're not currently saying but that you would share if you were being truly brave and standing in your power.

I once attended an interactive session on diversity and inclusion by unconscious bias experts Amy Lazarus and Emi Kolawole from InclusionVentures, who encouraged us to ask, "What are the uncomfortable things that need to be said in your workplace before a team or culture can truly change?" Inclusion can't happen until the unsaid is spoken. The audience can't transform until you say what you actually want to say.

# Interview with Cloe Shasha

"I'm looking for people who are doing work that matters."

Cloe Shasha is the director of speaker development for TED. She has worked at TED for seven years, and has been involved in curation and talk development of speakers for around 25 TED events, including TED in Vancouver, TEDWomen, TEDYouth, TEDGlobal, TED idea search events (where TED puts out an open call for applications), and small, themed events at the TED office in New York. She estimates that she has worked with nearly 800 TED speakers in some capacity, either through communications, editing, coaching, or the rehearsal process.

## How did you end up working at TED?

I organized the first TEDxMiddlebury at Middlebury College in 2010, and a very generous alum invited me to attend the TEDActive conference as a gift! I am still so grateful. I showed up for the conference in beautiful, sunny Palm Springs, California in the spring of my senior year. There, I ended up talking with my future boss in a swimming pool. We talked about my college studies and thesis research in psychology, her children, and New York City. She told me about a role she was looking to fill on her team and invited me to interview for it when I was home for spring break. The role was on a different team than the one I'm on now. Seven years later, I'm still at TED!

**What do you love about working at TED?**

What I love about my work at TED is that I'm always learning. When it comes to looking for speakers or working with speakers (for the stage or for a podcast), I love the opportunity to delve into someone's world and help them pull out what would be most interesting in a short talk. I love thinking about the arc, narrative, and flow of ideas. I also love the people I work with. My colleagues are incredible people and I consider many of them to be like family.

**Describe what you're looking for when you're considering speakers for TED events.**

I'm looking for people who are doing work that matters.

People who are getting their hands dirty (metaphorically speaking, but also, sometimes, literally! We've had several urban farmers on our stage). I'm looking for people who are the best in their fields—who are bringing something new to those fields, and working on ideas that are timely. I read articles they've written, coverage on them, watch videos, or listen to audio of them speaking. And I talk to people who know more about a speaker's particular field than I do (like my colleagues who are subject matter expert curators). I look for people who approach ideas from different perspectives, because we are always seeking a balance.

## What questions should speakers ask themselves if they want to improve their craft?

- What is the main idea I want to communicate in this talk?
- Who is my audience, and how does that matter with regards to how I talk about the key points in this talk?
- What supporting stories and data points can I include to communicate that idea?
- What are some specific takeaways I want to make sure people leave with?
- Where am I using generic language and how can I trim that back and replace it with strong sentences and phrases that hold more meaning?
- How am I most comfortable preparing for a talk? If

I'm good at memorizing, can I commit to starting that memorization process a couple of weeks before the talk?

- If I'm better at riffing off of a structured outline, can I practice my talk while holding that structure in my head enough times to feel super comfortable?
- If I'm going to be using slides, how can I ensure that every slide is truly going to complement what I'm saying in that moment of my talk rather than distract the audience from hearing what I'm saying?

## Do you have specific recommendations for how conferences can book more women, people of color, and other underrepresented people to speak?

Follow blogs and magazines that highlight underrepresented people's work, go to conferences that draw different demographics, go to award ceremonies, look at other organizations' fellows, and in general, have subject matter experts who know their fields so well that they know a wide variety of amazing people who could talk about a given issue in that field.

## Are there any critical resources that you recommend for speakers?

I mean, I work at TED, so I recommend checking out Chris Anderson's book: *TED Talks*. Chris also made a great little video about how to give a good talk: "Chris Anderson, TED's secret to great public speaking." I'd also recommend taking improvisational theater classes to get comfortable onstage, or singing lessons to improve the resonance of your voice. Listen to podcasts hosted by interviewers you deeply respect—hearing their use of language can remind us how to craft our words more thoughtfully. And then, honestly, just watch lots of great talks or lectures wherever you typically follow content!

**Connect with Cloe:** about.me/cloeshasha, @cloe_shasha

# 7

# Focus, focus, focus

**AS I WAS WRITING THIS SECTION,** a speaker reached out to me about getting a recommendation to speak at more events. I looked at his website, and his speaking topics included: "Innovation, entrepreneurship, social impact, diversity and inclusion, technology, leadership and motivation." I thought to myself, "What *doesn't* this dude speak about? There's no way he knows enough to be an expert in all of these subjects. He hasn't even done seven speaking gigs, and he has seven topics listed on his website!"

When you speak about everything, you speak about nothing.

Especially when you are getting started, the biggest mistake you can make is to assume you're qualified to speak about multiple topics. Pick one topic and become an expert in that area. Obviously, every talk you do will require you to cater your message slightly to the specific audience you're speaking to, but it's best to stay within one major topic, not three, and certainly not seven. No one is an expert in seven topics.

# 8

# Carve a niche, then carve a niche within your niche

**I CAN'T TELL YOU HOW MANY** speakers tell me they are a "leadership speaker." Or a "wellness speaker." Or an "innovation speaker." I have no idea what it means to be a "leadership speaker." This lack of specificity will guarantee you don't book a lot of gigs. Get as clear as possible on your niche. For example, I don't just speak about "millennials," I am a "millennial workplace expert" who speaks about "attracting, retaining, and engaging millennials in the workplace." Don't just be a "blockchain person," be a "blockchain in emerging markets expert" or a "women in cryptocurrency advocate." Don't just talk about "AI," talk about "why inclusive design matters for the future of AI" or "how AI is impacting the jobs crisis." Get as specific as possible on what you speak about, who your audience is, and why you're the right person to give a talk.

As you deepen your niche within your niche, practicing your one talk over and over again, your goal is to become the go-to person for your niche. Have you ever noticed on Facebook how certain people always get tagged in a thread about a specific topic? I have a friend named Meltem Demirors who is a cryptocurrency investor, advisor, and advocate. She's also the Chief Strategy Officer of CoinShares, which builds treasury management solutions for cryptocurrency companies to minimize financial risk and pioneer financial management strategies for blockchain networks. Whenever someone posts an article related to blockchain on my wall, sure enough, Mel is tagged in the comments. Not only does she usually respond to the person who tagged her, but she engages in a conversation about the article and what it means for the future of cryptocurrency. Who do you think people tag when they see a conference call for an awesome blockchain speaker? Mel.

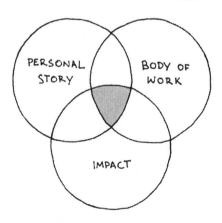

SPEAKER ZONE OF GENIUS

# Exercise: Your Speaker Zone of Genius

This is an exercise that will help you carve your niche. Make a list of at least **ten** topics you've spoken about or would like to speak about. This list should include everything you've ever dreamed you could speak about. You can get silly with your list. For example, my list includes "How to make the best potato latke ever," "How to dance pretty damn well, all things considered," and "If I ruled the world: kombucha, kale, and dance parties." Once you have your list, circle the **three** topics that are within your **Speaker Zone of Genius**. By **Speaker Zone of Genius**, I mean, your **Personal Story** (your life thus far, your narrative, what makes you unique), the topics you are most qualified to speak on based on your **Body of Work** (your career experience, education, accomplishments), and your **Impact** (the impact you want to make on the world, your future legacy). The intersection of your **Personal Story**, **Body of Work**, and **Impact** is your **Speaker Zone of Genius**. It's where you can naturally speak about something in a way that is authentic to who you are, what you've experienced, what you've researched, what you're good at, and what you want to accomplish in your life.

Now, as much as I want to speak about "How to dance pretty damn well, all things considered," that's just not in my Speaker Zone of Genius. Although, for reals, I've twice learned and performed the dance choreography for the "SORRY" music video by Justin Bieber. Oh, I can move it, baby. Anyway, once you have your three Speaker Zone of Genius topics, narrow it down to one topic that you want to build your speaking business around over the coming months. What is that main topic that truly reflects your story, experience, and mission? If you absolutely can't decide on one, play with two as you practice your talks, and see which one seems more authentic and natural for you. A good test for determining what your Speaker Zone of Genius is to ask your parents, siblings, partner, or your five closest friends what they think you should speak about. Chances are, they know you pretty well.

# 9

# Become a one-hit wonder

**I'M GOING TO LET YOU IN** on a little secret. Every single speaker I know who makes a living from public speaking does pretty much the same talk every time they go on stage. Sure, they switch up a few slides here and there, but their content is more or less the same every single talk. They might even switch up the title, or tell an event planner that they're going to do something different, but they're going to do their talk the way they always do their talk. Sometimes they do the same exact talk, word for word. Even the cadence of their voice, the way they tell each joke, where they are on stage, and their body language is exactly the same every single time.

I know, being a one-hit wonder has kind of a negative connation, like that song "Tubthumping" by Chumbawumba. We think of one-hit wonders as boring. But you know what? If that song comes on in a bar, guess what? 99 percent of people in the room start singing (and sure, I'll admit it, I kind of like that song).

It's not wrong to do the same talk every time you go on stage: it's exactly what the experts do. I used to feel guilty that I was delivering similar material at every talk. Then I started to realize that all of the speakers I admired were using their old material—and they had been in the game for five, and sometimes ten years! I once saw a speaker give the same opening talk for a social innovation conference four times in a row. Literally, his talk was identical every single time—he told the same jokes and hit the same exact beats every single performance. But you know what? He was the most popular speaker at that conference every single time.

If you have material that works, use it. Think of yourself like a stand-up comedian or a musician that has a hit song. Do you know how many times top comedians test their material before recording a Netflix special or performing at Madison Square Garden? Hundreds of times. You want to do your best material over and over again, until it becomes so good that everyone hears it on the radio and is like, "Dammit, Chumbawumba, again?!"

When you're getting started, practice one talk (not two talks, and definitely not five talks) over and over again, until you are making over $10,000 a gig. Then, and only then, should you worry about writing another talk. Even the legends who make $25,000 or $50,000 (or much more) per speaking gig pretty much have one talk—maybe the Simon Sineks or Brené Browns of the world have two or three talks by now—but they probably only had one talk when they first started.

# 10

# You need an anchor

**UNLESS YOU ARE THE GREATEST** storyteller to live (and even then), you'll need an anchor on which to build your public speaking career. People get booked to speak because they've done something special. Anchors can be things like writing a book, starting a successful company, working for an impactful organization, being an expert in a field, running an engaged community, launching a social movement or creative project—anything that demonstrates authority, accomplishment, and influence. If you don't have an anchor yet, spend the time it takes (sometimes it takes a year or two—or even five or ten years!) to craft your anchor. You can book a few speaking gigs without an anchor, but if you truly want to speak for money, the anchor is your ticket.

You might not know what your anchor is until you try a few things and see what works for you. You'll recall that I set out to be a writer, but realized that writing was actually a far better anchor for my speaking than it was a day job. While there are as many potential anchors as there are creative endeavors in the world, here are five common anchors and brief examples of how a few speakers I know leveraged them.

**5 anchors to build your speaking career**

1. Write something that matters
2. Build a community
3. Launch something really cool
4. Be a founder of an influential company, or have an important role at an influential company
5. Make an (actual) social impact

**1. Write something that matters (book, popular article, academic paper, manifesto)**

Examples:

- **Elle Luna:** Elle wrote a viral blog post on Medium called "The Crossroads of Should and Must," that was read by a quarter-million people. The post was an inspiring call to action for following your passion, and it was filled with her beautiful hand-drawn illustrations. The post led to a book deal with Workman Publishing, and now Elle is a sought-after speaker on art, creativity, and doing what you love. She has spoken at Google, Wisdom 2.0, Creative Mornings, and the Do Lectures.

- **Julie Lythcott-Haims:** The former Dean of Freshman at Stanford University, Julie wrote the *New York Times* bestselling book, *How to Raise an Adult*, which explored helicopter parenting and gave practical advice for how parents should raise their kids in the 21$^{st}$ century. She frequently speaks at universities, high schools, associations, conferences, and major events like TED.

- **Chelsea Rustrum:** Chelsea is the author of *It's a Shareable Life*, one of the first in-depth explorations of the sharing economy. Chelsea frequently speaks around the world at tech conferences, companies, and to anyone who is interested in the future of sharing and the new economy. Her book has also led to a lucrative consulting business in collaborative economic models and the blockchain space. Chelsea has spoken at PwC, TEDxMenloPark, Expo in Milan, Slush in Helsinki, and Ouishare in Paris, among many others.

2. **Build a community (in-person community, online community, leadership or personal development program)**

Examples:

- **Minda Harts:** Minda, who you read about earlier, is the founder of The Memo LLC, a career development company for women of color with the mission of motivating and encouraging women of color to achieve their personal and professional goals with balance, generosity, integrity, and resilience. The Memo hosts career boot camps that teach salary negotiation, career change, networking, and leadership development. Minda's work with The Memo led to a blossoming speaking career, which includes speaking and leading workshops at NYU Stern School of Business, Time, Inc., the Campaign for Black Male Achievement, the New York Public Library, and Western Illinois University. Minda's work has been featured in *Forbes, Essence,* and *The Guardian,* and she recently closed a book deal with Seal Press and launched a podcast called Secure the Seat.

- **Cam Adair:** Cam is the founder of Game Quitters, the world's largest support community for video game addiction, reaching 50,000 people per month in over 90 countries. Cam has used his expertise in building a community around overcoming addiction to grow a successful speaking career at places like TEDx, the Mental Health Commission of Canada, Renew Youth Summit in Dar es Salaam, Tanzania, and SHRM, the largest human resources conference in the world. Cam's work has been featured in dozens of media publications, like *BBC, ABC 20/20, Forbes,* and *VICE,* and his TEDx talk "The Surprising

Truth About Rejection" has over 600,000 views.

- **Kat Alexander:** Kat Alexander is a social entrepreneur and public health researcher on a mission to help people heal from trauma. She's the founder and CEO of Report It, Girl, a web platform helping survivors of sexual violence heal through storytelling, community, and resources, which already has 10,000 participants from over 90 countries. Kat speaks about cultivating resilience after trauma, and she has spoken at Kaiser Permanente, the Coalition Against Sexual and Domestic Abuse, the San Diego County District Attorney Office, and Azusa Pacific University, among many others.

3. **Launch something really cool (a social movement, activism campaign, product, experiential journey, artistic endeavor)**

Examples:

- **Debbie Sterling:** Debbie is a Stanford University engineering graduate and the founder of Goldie-Blox, a toy company that makes toys that teach girls engineering skills. GoldieBlox is disrupting the pink aisle in toy stores globally and challenging gender stereotypes with the world's first girl engineering character who now appears in toys, books, apps, videos, and merchandise. GoldieBlox has reached billions of consumers through being the first start-up with a Super Bowl commercial and a float in the Macy's Thanksgiving Day Parade, and in 2014 was named one of *Fast Company's* Most Innovative Companies. Debbie was named *TIME's* Person of the Moment and *Business Insider's* 30 Women Who are Changing the World, and she now speaks around the world about STEM, women and girls in tech, and creating an impact-driven business.

- **Jeff Kirschner:** Jeff is the founder of Litterati, a global community dedicated to eradicating litter one piece at a time. The Litterati app uses technology and data to help clean the planet, by allowing users to geo-tag pieces of garbage by location, tag corporate brands and common products, influencing corporations to find more sustainable practices. Jeff was accepted into the prestigious TED Residency, and his TED talk, "This app makes it fun to pick up litter," has been viewed over one million times on TED.com. He has spoken at companies like Google, Facebook and Uber, keynoted environmental summits at the Monterey Bay Aquarium and Keep America Beautiful, and spoken at leading universities like Stanford, MIT, and the University of Michigan.

- **Tristan Harris:** Tristan spent three years as a design ethicist at Google before leaving to launch the Center for Humane Technology, a nonprofit initiative working to reform the attention economy and ensure that people's time online is Time Well Spent. The Center for Humane Technology aims to catalyze a coordinated change among technology companies to protect the public from addiction and manipulation. After a decade of research on addiction, persuasive design, and behavioral economics, Tristan is currently developing a framework for ethical persuasion as it relates to the moral responsibility of tech companies. He was named one of the 25 People Shaping the World in 2017 by *Rolling Stone*, and Tristan has been interviewed on RealTime with Bill Maher, 60 Minutes, and PBS NewsHour. Tristan's TED talks both have over one million views on TED. com, he regularly speaks at conferences around the world, and he has even briefed heads of state and members of U.S. Congress about the attention economy. In November 2017, Mark Zuckerberg made "time well spent" the new design goal for Facebook after four years of advocacy from Tristan and his colleagues.

4.  **Be a founder of an influential company, or have an important role at an influential company**

Examples:

- **Amy Lazarus:** Amy is the founder and CEO of InclusionVentures, a consulting firm that helps organizations bring out the best in their people so that, together they can bring their world-changing ideas to life. From assessments to executive sessions, train-the-trainer and facilitation, InclusionVentures creates learning experiences to help organizations take an inclusive approach to diversity, inclusion, workforce development, and leadership. Amy's work has been cited in numerous publications and she is a recipient of USA Network's Characters Unite Award, Top 99 Under 33 Foreign Policy Leaders, Facing History's Upstander Award, and the American Express NGen Leadership Fellowship. Amy is a frequent facilitator at top conferences, and her speaking and workshop engagements include Deloitte, Hewlett Packard, Pandora, TEDx, the World Economic Forum in Davos, Stanford's Design School, The White House, and Clinton Global Initiative.

- **Justin Rosenstein:** Justin is the co-founder of the work management software company Asana. Justin is an advocate for creating a mindful, compassionate, and purpose-driven workplace, and Asana was recently named one of *Inc.'s* Best Workplaces 2018, and one of *Fortune's* Great Places to Work 2018. By creating both a high-performing, fast-growing business and an award-winning, mission-driven workplace culture, Justin has been propelled into a high-demand speaker at top business and tech conferences. Justin's recent speaking engagements include Collision Conference, Lean Startup Week, Startup Grind Global, Wisdom 2.0, Chicago Ideas Week, Web Summit, The Culture Conference, and TechCrunch Disrupt.

- **Lisa Lee:** Lisa was the former director of diversity and inclusion strategies at Pandora, and recently became the director of diversity, inclusion, and community at Squarespace. A self-proclaimed "diversity geek," Lisa spends her time thinking about how to use tech as a vehicle to drive equality. Her role as an intrapreneur at Pandora oversaw diversity and inclusion, employee experience, giving, and university programs, and allowed her to help a beloved company reflect the diversity of its listeners, artists, and local communities. Passionate about uplifting the Asian American community, Lisa co-founded the positive body image site ThickDumplingSkin.com and served on the board of Asian Americans for Civil Rights and Equality and the National Asian Pacific American Women's Forum. Lisa is a frequent speaker on panels and conferences, and she's presented at SXSW, General Assembly, The Future of Work Conference, Culture Summit, and has been interviewed on NPR.

## 5. Make an (actual) social impact

Examples:

- **Lauren Burke:** Lauren is a serial social entrepreneur, activist, and lawyer. She is a *Forbes* 30 Under 30 in Law and Policy, a 2014 Echoing Green fellow, a NYU Distinguished Young Alumni, a New York Law Journal Rising Star, and a New Leaders Council 40 Under 40. She is the founder of Atlas: DIY, a Brooklyn-based nonprofit that provides immigrant youth with access to legal services, leadership development, and learning opportunities, in a space run and governed by youth. In 2017, following the inauguration of Donald Trump, she and her friend Martina Carrillo completed a six-month road trip across America to provide free, on-demand legal services to immigrants and their communities, while documenting immigrant stories. Lauren now consults with organizations on curriculum design, programs, and start-up operations, facilitates retreats and boot camps for college students interested in social entrepreneurship, and is founding her first for-profit company called CaseNotes, software for everyone who takes notes on humans. In 2016, Lauren was diagnosed with Bipolar 2 disorder and has since become a national advocate to diminish stigma and was featured in the Demi Lovato-produced documentary *Beyond Silence*. Lauren has spoken about social entrepreneurship and leadership at many universities, law schools, organizations, and conferences.

- **Tiffany Yu:** Tiffany is a speaker, diversity and inclusion community builder, and empowerment advocate. She is the CEO and founder of Diversability, and an advocate for women in leadership and disability inclusion. She previously worked in corporate finance, including in investment banking at Goldman Sachs, where she worked on over $14 billion of announced transactions. Tiffany has spoken at many universities, TEDx, the World Economic Forum, Creative Mornings, Singularity University, StartingBloc, and Wonder Woman Tech, and her work has been featured in *Marie Claire*, *Forbes*, *The Wall St. Journal*, and *Fortune*.

- **Nikita Mitchell:** Nikita speaks and writes about why CEOs need to think beyond the bottom line. She is the creator of Above the Bottom Line, a newsletter showcasing how the world's most influential companies are taking a stance on social and environmental issues. Nikita received her MBA from UC Berkeley's Haas School of Business where she was a Principal of the Haas Socially Responsible Investment Fund, a $2.5 million student-led investment fund, and the Haas MBA Association's first black female president. Nikita is currently a senior manager at Cisco responsible for strategy and planning initiatives for the company's $20 billion Americas Sales organization, and serves on the board of trustees for Planned Parenthood Northern California. Nikita has spoken about corporate social responsibility, diversity, women in tech, and discovering your truth, at top business and tech conferences around the country.

# 11

# Align your Speaker Zone of Genius, Anchor, Hook, and Pain Point

**REMEMBER IN THE PREVIOUS** exercise how you identified your Speaker Zone of Genius by finding the intersection of your Personal Story, Body of Work, and Impact? Breakthrough Speakers are able to align their unique **Speaker Zone of Genius** with their **Anchor** (something that establishes authority, accomplishment, and influence), a **Hook**, and a **Pain Point**. A Hook is a highly-relevant, newsworthy, top-of-mind topic that people care about, and a Pain Point is an issue that directly impacts a company or organization's day-to-day business.

Without all four of these lining up, it's hard to make serious money in public speaking. You might be very experienced and knowledgeable about a subject, and you might even have an anchor like a published book, but if it's lacking a Hook, meaning it's not something top-of-mind, or it's not solving a Pain Point, addressing something companies care about, you're not going to book a lot of speaking gigs. Similarly, if you're super-experienced in your field, and you speak about something that a lot of people are talking about, and that organizations are focusing on, but you're lacking an Anchor that proves your authority and influence, it's going to be hard to book gigs.

Visually, this looks like;

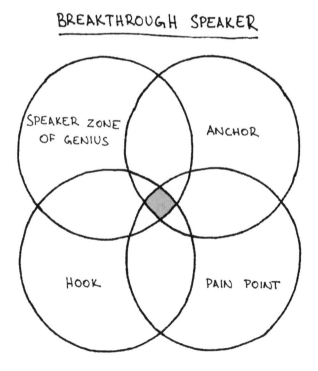

So, where do your Speaker Zone of Genius, Anchor, Hook, and Pain Point meet? That's the place where your speaking career will blossom. I should note that in addition to all four of these aligning, you also need to be a talented public speaker, but I assume you've already got that one dialed!

Let's take a look at a few examples. My Speaker Zone of Genius is helping 20-somethings find meaningful work; my Anchor was publishing *The Quarter-Life Breakthrough*; the Hook is that millennials are now the largest generation in the workplace; and the Pain Point is that millennial turnover costs U.S. companies $30 billion a year. Organizations are desperately trying to figure out how to retain top millennial talent and foster intergenerational collaboration.

Julie Lychott-Haims' Speaker Zone of Genius is advising parents how to raise productive adults, and her Anchor is two-fold—being the former Dean of Freshman at Stanford University and writing the *New York Times* bestseller *How to Raise an Adult*. Her Hook is the trend of helicopter parenting, and her Pain Point is that parents desperately want to know how to help their children succeed.

Amy Lazarus' Speaker Zone of Genius is creating inclusive cultures; her Anchor is launching a company that works with large and small organizations on their challenges with diversity and inclusion; her Hook is that diversity, inclusion, and belonging is something few organizations do well (not to mention something that our country is currently deeply divided by); and her Pain Point is that companies with more diverse workforces are proven to perform better, and organizations are losing top employees, specifically women and people of color, because they haven't created inclusive or supportive cultures.

Justin Rosenstein's Speaker Zone of Genius is how to be a mindful, compassionate leader; his Anchor is being the co-founder of Asana, which was named the best culture in tech by *Fast Company*; his Hook is that employees are increasingly seeking meaning and purpose from their work; and his Pain Point is that organizations know that if they're better at creating thriving cultures, their employees will perform better and the organizations will succeed more.

# 12

# Heal corporate pain

**A LOT OF PEOPLE THINK I BOOK** speaking gigs because I'm a really engaging speaker. This is only partially true. The real reason I book speaking gigs is because I'm an engaging speaker who is talking about a very real problem many organizations are facing: how to retain millennial employees at their company, how to make sure millennials and older generations collaborate respectfully and productively in the workplace, and how companies can create a culture where all employees feel heard and valued in the workplace. These are top-of-mind issues for my clients. They also happen to be issues that major publications like *Fast Company*, *Wired*, and *Harvard Business Review* frequently cover.

I once received a great piece of unsolicited advice from Richie Etwaru, a blockchain speaker I met at a gig in Europe. Richie has been chief digital officer for Quintilies IMS, head of Innovation at UBS Wealth Management, and a Senior VP at Lehman Brothers. He teaches block-chain management at Syracuse University, is the author of *Blockchain: Trust Companies: Every Company Is at Risk of*

*Being Disrupted by a Trusted Version of Itself*, and regularly speaks around the world on the future of blockchain and cryptocurrency. Richie saw my talk and thought it was good, but he advised me to make sure I tied my content to financial imperatives faced by companies. As Richie put it, "Don't just talk about how millennials are great. Focus on how costly millennial turnover is for organizations. And how employee engagement saves companies money."

In my future talks, I incorporated Richie's feedback, which was well-received. Millennial turnover costs the U.S. economy $30 billion a year. At the end of the day, companies care about making and saving money. *You care* about purpose and impact. Companies say they care about purpose and impact (and the good ones actually do). But they really care about performance. Your job is to tie the work you're doing around purpose and impact to the bottom-line issues companies are facing around performance, productivity, and profit. How will recruiting more diverse talent lead to an increase in performance, tenure, and new ideas? How will investing in professional development or building a more purpose-driven culture lead to an increase in profit and growth? How will creating meditation or wellness programs save a company in health care costs or improve employee well-being and productivity?

For example, I once met a brilliant speaker at Dreamforce named Haben Girma. Haben speaks about disability and innovation, and what she believes are the "universal benefits of inclusive design." Haben is the first Deafblind person to graduate from Harvard Law School. President Obama named her a White House Champion of Change, she is a *Forbes* 30 under 30, and is writing a memoir to be published by Hachette in 2019. Haben speaks around the world, teaching others about the benefits of fully accessible products and services.

Now, you might not think that advocating for equal opportunities for people with disabilities is something corporations actually care about, but Haben makes her value proposition for clients crystal clear, explaining, "People with disabilities represent the largest minority group, numbering one billion worldwide. Reaching a group of this scale creates value for everyone. Organizations that prioritize accessibility benefit by gaining access to a much larger user base, improving the experience for both disabled and non-disabled users, and facilitating further innovation."

In short, how can you tie your talk to the pain points organizations are facing? How can you solve problems your clients are facing? Wanabee Speakers like to talk about how great they are, but Breakthrough Speakers add value. Breakthrough Speakers provide solutions. As my friend and fellow workplace engagement speaker Antonio Neves says, "Public speaking isn't for the speaker, it's for the audience... Learn what your client wants so you can meet their needs. Ask them what success looks like."

# 13

# Take advantage of trends and timeliness

**BREAKTHROUGH SPEAKERS,** in addition to being talented, talk about something that is timely and trendy. The more your topic has a Hook, the more it is a top-of-mind issue in the media and workplace, the more likely you are to be booked. The challenge is that we live in a 24-hour news cycle dominated by a president who tweets as often as a toddler cries, and by the time you're reading this, today's key issues might be yesterday's garbage. You might think you're talking about a trendy topic, only to realize you're late to the party. This happened to me with the Future of Work topic. I thought everyone wanted to hear me talk about the Future of Work, only to realize people had been sitting through the same Future of Work talk at conferences *for three whole years*. They were tired of that shit! I had to find a new angle.

As of mid-2018, here are a few top-of-mind issues my communities are talking about:

- How to get diversity and inclusion right in the workplace
- How to increase the number of women in leadership roles across industries
- How to end sexual harassment in the workplace; the impact of #MeToo on the workplace, business, tech, entertainment, media, and leadership
- How to fix toxic masculinity; how to increase emotional well-being for men, especially young men; the relationship between toxic masculinity and gun violence
- How to decrease anxiety and depression rates; the growing mental health epidemic; the loneliness epidemic and the need for in-person community
- The opioid epidemic
- How to solve humanity's growing dependency and addiction to tech
- Tech's privacy and data challenges
- How to fix the "bubble" problem caused by Facebook and social media
- The relationship between free speech and safe spaces on college campuses
- How to increase empathy among people who strongly disagree
- How blockchain and cryptocurrencies will change business and commerce
- The need for universal basic income
- How AI is shaping the future of work; how people will work and live when the robots take over
- The rise of Gen-Z and the Smartphone Generation

- How to solve the most serious issues of our time, like climate change, income inequality, mass migration, access to affordable health care, housing and education, systemic injustices, poverty, and access to critical resources like water and food
- How to apply design thinking and systems thinking to the most serious challenges of our time; how to design for sustainability and social good.

What are your communities talking about? What articles have you been reading lately, or seen shared multiple times on your news feed? If you're having trouble booking gigs, especially in the corporate arena, try latching on to a major trend, and once that trend starts to fade, predict the next one.

As important as it is to latch onto a major trend or timely topic of conversation, you can't fake it. If you're not the best person to talk about an issue, the audience is going to smell your opportunistic and inauthentic play from a mile away. Remember to come back to who you are and why you started speaking in the first place. A speaking agent who has been in the business for more than twenty years once told me, "The best speakers have a fire burning inside them. I don't want to hear a speaker who wants to tell me something about a hot topic. I want to hear a speaker who has a fire burning within, something they have to share."

What's burning inside you? Chances are, it's not going away anytime soon. In Part II, we'll learn how to take this fire burning from within you and make it contagious.

# PART II.
# SHARE
# YOUR TRUTH

# 14

# The life-changing magic of giving a TED talk

**THE SINGLE MOST IMPORTANT** talk I've given in my speaking career thus far was my TEDx talk, which was hosted by TEDxYouth@MileHigh at the Ellie Caulkins Opera House in Denver, Colorado. I remember walking into the 2,000-seat Opera House for rehearsal the day before the event, thinking to myself, *holy shit, how am I gonna pull this one off?!* I was nervous as hell looking at all those empty seats. Good thing I did all those visioning exercises, imagining that I was at the Oscars: when the lights blinded me on stage during rehearsal, I felt like I was giving my acceptance speech. I barely slept the night before the event, and then found out my talk wasn't until 4:45pm. I was the last speaker of the day. I had another freak out—how the hell was I going to sit through the rest of the talks?!

After going for a run in the morning, I began to

relax. The cool thing about TEDxYouth events is that the audience is filled with local high school students. I introduced myself to several groups of students in the exhibition hall and realized, *wow, these kids are awesome!* If you ever are nervous before a gig, just go sit in the audience and introduce yourself to a few people—chances are you'll feel a lot more relaxed.

When I finally took the stage at 4:45pm in front of a packed house of more than 2,000 people, I was ready. Or, almost ready. I was in the bathroom when they called my name, but I ran to the stage just in time! My TEDx talk, "Refusing to Settle: The Quarter-Life Crisis" now has over 450,000 views on YouTube. It's the video I usually share with people who have never seen me speak before, and it's the single-largest driver of traffic to my website after my book. All of which is to say: do whatever you have to do to get a TEDx talk. Here are a few ways to do that:

1. Search the TEDx website for TEDx events in your area. Most events have a website and a contact form where you can contact the organizer or apply to speak. There are five TEDx events happening every single day in 130 countries, so you should be able to find a TEDx event near you that fits your schedule and subject matter.

2. A better option than applying via a TEDx website is finding a TEDx organizer in your network. One

option is posting on your Facebook wall: "Hi everyone, I've been doing a lot of public speaking and I'm ready to give a TEDx talk. Please let me know if you know of someone organizing an event."

3. An even better option is to find a friend who has spoken at a TEDx event you want to speak at, and then message your friend, asking them to introduce you to the TEDx organizer. This is exactly how I booked my TEDx talk in Denver. The previous year, my friend Evan Walden had spoken at TEDx-MileHigh, and I asked him to introduce me to the organizer, who agreed to invite me to speak based on Evan's recommendation.

One more thing: TEDx talks normally do not pay their speakers or cover their expenses. I even had to pay for my own flight to Denver. Was it worth it? Every single penny.

# 15

# Never underestimate your audience

**SPEAKING TO AN AUDITORIUM** of 2,000 high school students taught me an essential lesson I've remembered ever since: stay humble. A few people gave me the (bad) advice that high school students would not understand my TEDx talk, and that I should remove my references to Facebook-induced FOMO and struggling with career anxiety and how to find a job in your twenties. I didn't listen to this advice, and I'm grateful I didn't. It turns out high school students can strongly relate to being jealous of their friends on social media and freaking out about what to do with their lives. In fact, the students were so engaged that I had to pause twice during my talk for audience applause and laughter.

Never assume that your audience isn't old enough or smart enough to understand what you're talking about. Your audience might even know more than you about your topic! Treat your audience like peers, even and especially if you are talking to kids. I did another TEDxYouth talk in 2016 that was in a middle school library for about 30 people, mostly 5th and 6th graders. The previous month, I had keynoted a conference in Stockholm with over a thousand people in the audience, three movie theater-sized HD screens behind me, and fancy stage lights, where they even gave me an intro song as I walked on stage (the theme song for *Game of Thrones*!)—I felt like Arya Stark up there.

But there I was, a few weeks later, giving a talk in a middle school library to a bunch of 5th graders. It turned out to be one of the most meaningful talks I've ever done. I spoke about how my grandmother was the best life coach I ever had, and how it made no sense that every life coach I saw on Instagram posted photos of themselves perfectly tan, usually on a beach, doing yoga all the time. "It's like, who the hell has time to do yoga every second of every day?!" The 5th graders were loving it. A good rule of thumb: if a 5th grader (and their parents) can relate to your talk, then you're in good shape.

# 16

# It's all about the video

**THERE ARE A LOT OF REASONS** to give a TEDx talk, including practicing on a formal stage and the credibility that comes with speaking on that circular red carpet. People see that you've done a TEDx talk and immediately take you more seriously as a speaker. But less people realize that the real reason to give a TEDx talk is the video. Most TEDx events hire professional videographers and audio teams, and all TEDx talks are uploaded on YouTube, which increases the chance that people you've never met before, from all over the world, can watch you speak. In addition, it means you have a high-quality video to put on your website—that you don't even have to pay for.

My friend Cam Adair runs a community called Game Quitters, dedicated to helping people break free of their addiction to video games. He gave a talk at TEDxBoulder called "Escaping video game addiction" that now has over 275,000 views. This talk helped him launch his speaking career at colleges and conferences around the world, and even allowed Cam to book a second TEDxFargo talk called "The surprising truth about rejection" (which has over 600,000 views).

# 17

# What happens if you can't get a TEDx talk?

**IF YOU CAN'T FIND A TEDX** event to speak at, have no fear. As I mentioned, the video is the most important part, so just host your own event and hire a professional videographer to record your talk. Find a friend's office or event space, put together an invite on Facebook or Eventbrite, invite your friends, practice your talk, and when the time comes, make sure you capture a high-quality video of your talk! This also works as a good back-up plan if you've given a TEDx talk, but you aren't happy with your performance. If you really want to have fun with this, invite your friends to speak as well! My friend George did this once for his birthday and asked all of his friends to deliver 1-minute talks about him— he called it GEORGEx.

In addition to TEDx, there are a number of other local events that are always looking for speakers and storytellers, including Toastmasters, Ignite, and The Moth. Or, try going to an open-mic night and sharing your story. If there's not an open-mic in your hometown, create one yourself! My friend Molly Sonsteng hosts an event in New York City called First Time Out, which is a variety show for first-time performers. If you're scared of getting on stage, the best place to go is a place where everyone else is just as nervous.

## Exercise: Host your own dream event

This exercise is particularly useful if you're a new speaker that needs to get more video footage for your website and speaker reel, but it's a fun activity for veteran speakers as well. For this exercise, plan your own dream event. Pick a date a month or so from now. Find a venue you love that you can get for free that will fit 10 of your friends. Possibilities include your office, a friend's office, your local café, an art gallery, or your friend's apartment. If you can't find a venue, host it in your living room. Make a Facebook event page or Eventbrite for your event. Name your dream event, invite your friends and let them know you'll be speaking at the event. If you want to get fancy, invite a few of your friends to speak as well!

Think about the vibe you want to create for your event. Do you want to provide a specific kind of food or beverage? What about décor or music? Is there an activity you want to lead before your talk begins? Think about how you want your friends (the audience) to feel after the event is over. Being intentional about your event will help you think about how you present yourself—and being a better host will make you a better speaker. Pro tip: remember to find someone to record a video of you speaking! Bonus points: before your event is over, ask your friends for feedback about your talk. What moments stood out? What did they think you did well? Where can you improve? What was missing from your talk?

## 18

# Build a personal website with the essentials

**IF YOU WANT TO BOOK PAID** speaking gigs, you need to have a website, period. Sometimes, I want to recommend a friend for a panel or speaking gig, but when I ask them for their website, they don't have one and they give me their LinkedIn. It's possible to book a panel from a LinkedIn page, but it's very difficult to get a keynote (let alone a paid keynote) without a website. The point is that you want to make it as easy as possible for a conference organizer or company to learn who you are, what you speak about, where you've spoken before, and what it's like to see you speak. Websites do this far more effectively than a LinkedIn page.

Note: if you're the CEO of a start-up or run an organization, it is not enough to send the organizer your company's website. Think about it: does a company website have your speaking reel or say anything about what a 30-minute talk by you includes? Nope. I don't care if you work for Facebook or The White House (well, if you're Sheryl Sandberg or Barack Obama, you probably don't need a website—but you ain't Barack Obama! And yes, I realize Barack Obama doesn't work at The White House anymore—I'm still in denial).

If you want to get paid to speak, make a personal website. The website can be simple (I recommend using Squarespace to make simple, clean, good-looking websites), but your website should include these essentials:

- A domain name that's easily searchable in Google (first name, last name). A lot of speakers have a domain that's a brand or a coaching company or something like that, which is a mistake. It's far better for SEO purposes to have your website just be your full name.
- Your name and title
- Your bio
- What you speak about in a few words (1 sentence maximum)
- What you speak about in greater detail (1-2 paragraphs maximum)
- A video reel or links to the best videos of your talks
- A few high-res photos of you speaking
- Logos of all the companies where you've spoken
- A list of any past events where you've spoken and any upcoming events

- Testimonials from people who have booked you to speak
- Links to any press clips of your work
- Your social media links
- A subscribe button so people can sign up for your email newsletter
- A contact form so people can invite you to speak

# 19

# All you need is 3

**SPEAKERS WHO ARE JUST** beginning their career often worry that they don't have enough material to start booking paid speaking gigs. My advice is to take a deep breath and remember that "all you need is 3 speaking opportunities." These don't have to be paid. They can be a lunch-and-learn at your friend's office, a free meet-up at a coworking space, a talk you're giving at your local General Assembly or WeWork, or a local Toastmasters event—basically anywhere where you're in front of a room talking. At each of the three gigs, get a video, photos, and a testimonial. After having zero material on your website, suddenly you have three videos, three logos of places you've spoken, three testimonials, and maybe even three guest posts at websites where you wrote about your talk. You're well on your way. Not satisfied with one of your three talks? I mean, how could you be, you've only given three talks! This is a perfect reason to go out and do a fourth talk—and now you can replace the first video you have on your site (which was kind of weak), with the fourth talk that was much better.

# Exercise: Find a mission-aligned brand or partner organization

In my first book, *The Quarter-Life Breakthrough*, I wrote about the power of partnering with mission-aligned brands and organizations to advance your career goals. This tool is especially useful in the speaking industry. Now that you've practiced hosting your own dream event in your living room, it's time to organize an event with a mission-aligned partner. For example, when I was building my speaking career, I frequently spoke at General Assembly. General Assembly is an innovative modern-day school for adults, with locations around the world that offers coding, product management, design, and other technology-related classes. Now, I don't speak about web design or technology, but GA and I happen to share the same audience: 20- and 30-somethings who are hungry for meaning, interested in career development and finding meaningful work. Every time I did an event at GA, I got to speak in front of dozens of millennials that I would otherwise be unable to reach with my message. Not only that, but every time I spoke at GA, they would blast their email list with thousands of subscribers about my work, so even if people weren't showing up at my talk, they could still click on my website and buy my book.

So, what are some brands and organizations you can partner with to host a speaking event? Make a list of the leading organizations in your industry and reach out to them about creating a mission-aligned partnership.

# 20

# Make a speaker reel

**AFTER YOU'VE DONE A NUMBER** of speaking gigs, you'll want to edit a short 2-3 minute speaker reel with clips from your talks. The main reason you need a reel is that conference organizers and corporate bookers are very busy. Once, a speaking agent asked me to send them a video clip of me speaking to share with a client that he thought might be interested in me, and I sent the agent a link to my 15-minute TED talk and another YouTube link to a 32-minute keynote I gave. The agent came back and said bluntly, "This video is 30-minutes too long." So, I paid my friend who is a video editor to edit together the best clips of me speaking into a reel. A good speaker reel should answer several questions for the client in three minutes or less:

- Who are you?
- Why do you have any authority to speak?
- What does the client get when they book you? What's your Speaker Zone of Genius? What's your Anchor? What's the Hook? Why does your talk matter? How

will your talk make an organization better?

- What's your speaking style on the stage? Are you (actually) a good speaker? Can you prove that you're good in three minutes?

How important is your reel for booking a gig? According to some experts, it's the single most important marketing asset you have. Recently, I attended 3 Ring Circus, a boot camp for corporate speakers to grow their speaking business. 3 Ring Circus is organized by Josh Linkler, an innovation and creativity speaker, who has been the founder and CEO of five tech companies, and is the author of two *New York Times* bestsellers, *Disciplined Dreaming* and *The Road to Reinvention*.

Josh has been speaking for many years, his keynote fee is $35,000, and he regularly speaks 125 times a year—so he knows what he's doing. Josh told me and the other speakers at 3 Ring Circus that your video should be as powerful as you on stage—and that you should invest whatever your speaking fee is into your reel. For example, if you get paid $5000 to give a talk, you should be spending $5000 on your reel. When I heard this advice, I felt embarrassed because I only spent $300 on my reel. When I got home after the training, I wrote down on a Post-it, "Make a new speaker reel!"

# Exercise: Get feedback

Your speaking reel is going to be the main video you send to potential clients, so you want it to be as strong as possible. A good way to do this is to send it around to a few friends (and clients that have booked you to speak before) and ask for feedback. What was their favorite part of your reel? What was the worst part? Does your reel authentically communicate who you are? What's missing from your reel? I once heard a member of Pixar Animation Studios' leadership team share that Pixar frequently hosts screenings of its movies that are works-in-progress, inviting everyone in the office to give feedback, regardless of whether they're even working on the movie. Even the accountants and the kitchen staff are invited. Pixar believes that good ideas come from anywhere, and that every work of art—yes, even *Coco* and *Inside Out*—can be improved. If *Coco* can be improved, so can your speaking reel.

# Interview with Monica Kang

"Create allies in as many places as you can."

Monica Kang is the founder and CEO of InnovatorsBox, a creative education firm in Washington, D.C., that catalyzes sustainable change at the level where it matters the most: your mindset. She speaks about creativity for professionals who have no time, unlocking daily creativity and innovation, and social entrepreneurship. Monica speaks at Fortune 500 companies, conferences and universities, and she has delivered around 100 speaking engagements in the past year or two.

## Why did you start public speaking?

I speak because I want to inspire, motivate and encourage others to go beyond. Knowing how far I have gone as a self-taught speaker motivates me to speak up and hopefully inspire more self-taught future speakers who are ready to share their inspirational message to the world. In addition to my actual message, I'm excited to speak each time because I know I'm given the opportunity to represent a voice that is often underrepresented and may not have the stage to present: young, female, and Asian.

## How did you improve your talk over time?

I take a lot of time to study my audience, their expectations, the venue, and what is going on in the organization that may impact their interest and disinterest as well. It helps significantly to keep in mind where my work comes into context with their day, week and year, so I focus on getting to know as much as I can about the audience. Sometimes if it's related to creative mindset, I ask clients or participants to fill out a survey so that I learn more about them.

The second thing I emphasize is the interactive element. I don't want to do a simple lecture style. Even if the message is powerful, I want to take advantage of being "offline" and in the present moment by getting everyone involved in-person and excited about thinking differently. At times, I see myself more as the facilitator than a speaker who is finding new ways to spark their curiosity. Hence, I focus on creating a flow that is engaging the participants through my products like SPARK, or other materials like crayon, paper, Post-its, and Sharpies.

I spend a lot of time before and after my engagement to see how things went: what worked, what didn't, what did people say, how did people respond, how do I feel about it, was it worth spending that much time or should I have spent more time on something else. I also always try to invite someone I know such as a team member, mentor, or friend who I can rely on to get critical feedback as well as someone who may have seen me in previous events to see how I am doing in comparison to that.

## What's your advice for a new speaker trying to book their first few speaking engagements?

- **Focus on quality over quantity.** While it's great to book a lot of gigs, if you do a pretty bad job, you're less likely to be asked back. Your ideal scenario is to be asked back, referred to and have people loving how much you have created a unique experience. Spend more time making that one experience something people will want to remember and find a way to make the most out of it each time.

- **Think about the topics you are asked to do versus the topic you want to be representing**. If they are different, you may want to think about it. Saying yes to any speaking gig may not help you position or brand yourself in a helpful way. That being said, if you are looking for a new direction, you may want to be willing to start with low expectations so that you can build over time.

- **Be aware of how much you can "give" at a low cost.** If there is no clear gain from speaking, it may not be the right fit. While being paid is the ideal scenario, not every company may be in the situation to pay due to their constraints. Be mindful how often or for whom you may be willing to do that pro-bono gig and even if you do, what are things you can barter and ask for, so that you are being strategic. Are you going to get a great testimonial, introduction, opportunity to attend an event where you connect with more clients?

**Who are speakers you know that you love watching?**

Raeha Kim, Kimberly Moore, Melanie Spring, Tiffany Yu, Antionette Carroll, Shinjini Das.

**Connect with Monica:** Innovatorsbox.com, Twitter: @monicahkang, Instagram: hi.mhk

## 21

# Social media alone will not get you speaking gigs

**I MENTIONED IN THE INTRODUCTION** that I don't have a huge social media following. Especially when you're just starting out, my advice is to focus less on your social media presence and more on building your anchor. What is the one thing people are going to remember you by, that will make them want to invite you to speak somewhere? Your book? Your company? Your podcast? Your cool job? Chances are, it's not your Instagram feed. Millennial and Gen-Z speakers sometimes have a hard time understanding this. I meet a lot of aspiring young speakers who are jealous of me when I tell them what I earn from speaking. Once someone actually said to me, "Smiley: I have 20,000 Instagram followers, and you only have 2,000 Instagram followers. I should be booking more speaking gigs than you."

I replied, "What's your anchor?" He looked at me

with a blank expression on his face.

Once you have an anchor, focus on building a really good personal website. I asked the same kid with all the Instagram followers to show me his website. He didn't have one. And he didn't have a video of him speaking either. Instagram won't book you speaking gigs. A strong anchor, a solid website, and a good video will. At the 3 Ring Circus speaker training I mentioned, Josh Linkler advised that you should be spending three times as much time and energy on your website as you do on social media.

In order of priority, I recommend taking these actions:

1. Create an anchor people care about
2. Build a personal website
3. Get a high-quality video of you speaking (when you have 3-4 videos, make a speaker reel)
4. Pick 1-2 social media channels to focus on for your content

One of my favorite thought leaders, author and computer science professor Cal Newport doesn't even use social media, and believes that's the reason he was able to write influential books like *So Good They Can't Ignore You* and *Deep Work*. Cal believes that social media keeps people from focusing and creating their best work—in other words, while being active on social media, it's hard to find the time necessary to actually build your anchor. I'm hesitant to advise you to give up social media all together, because I do believe posting photos and stories of my journey to becoming a writer and speaker has helped me reach my audience and book gigs (and hopefully has inspired others to become writers and speakers as well). But I do agree with Cal that all of us would be better off if we used social media less.

Once you have a strong anchor and a solid website, social media is an incredible tool to share your message and connect with potential speaking leads. But, you don't have to be active on every single app. Focus on the one platform where your audience spends the most time. If you're speaking to Gen-Zers and high school students, Snapchat is more effective than Facebook. I once asked a room full of college students if they would follow me on Facebook. They were like, "Facebook is what our parents use! We don't have Facebook!" I felt so old! If you're an interior designer, focus on Instagram or Pinterest. But if you're trying to reach human resource officers, recruiters or sales experts, LinkedIn (not Facebook or Instagram) is probably where the party's at.

# 22

# Spread your message across multiple mediums

**AFTER YOU HONE IN ON YOUR** message, topic, and audience, you'll want to share this message in articles, slides, photos, blog posts, podcasts, website interviews—any and every chance you get. The goal is to create an echo chamber across the Internet where your name is being paired with your subject expertise as much as possible, as frequently as possible. This echo chamber across the Internet ends up improving your SEO (search-engine optimization), and increases the likelihood that when people search for speakers in your subject, your website comes up.

People often ask me how I get inbound speaking requests. The short answer is that when you do a Google search for "millennial workplace expert," my website comes up on the first page, ranked at number two. This is awesome. I'd like to think that everyone is booking me to speak because they think I'm charming and ridiculously funny, but the real reason is that they are lazy and my website was one of a few they had the time to glance at. Improving your SEO rank takes time. I've written dozens and dozens of articles and been interviewed numerous times by publications, which all add up to the fact that "Adam Smiley Poswolsky" and "millennial workplace expert" appear on the Internet hundreds of times together. That's the result of four years of hard work, and it's the reason why I make money speaking.

## Exercise: Do a content review

As you build your speaking career, it's helpful to get a sense of everything you've produced so far. Do a Google search of your name and make a list of all the professional content you've created: articles, projects, podcasts, videos, slides, presentations, etc. Make a list of the keywords and themes that appear in your content. Is there anything you notice about your content? Is it all about one topic or six different topics? How often are you producing new content? Are you posting new articles or videos on a regular basis, or only every few months? For bonus points, share your content review with a friend and ask them to highlight the one piece of content you've made that stands out the most. Ask your friend why they find this piece of content so powerful.

# 23

# Write guest posts

**ONE OF THE BEST WAYS** to demonstrate your Speaker Zone of Genius is by writing guest posts for relevant publications in your field. A good guest post should accomplish several things:

1. **Demonstrate your experience and Speaker Zone of Genius.** Prove you know what you're talking about.

2. **Offer solutions.** Show you have practical solutions to a significant social problem, or know how to solve the challenges a company, organization, or an employee is facing.

3. **Get people excited about your message.** Write a piece that makes readers curious about hearing more stories from you. At the very least, they'll follow you on social media or sign up for your email newsletter. In some cases, they'll visit your website and see that you offer speaking and workshops, and BOOM, you've just converted a reader into a speaking lead.

4. **Open the door for further conversation.** Be sure to include a link to your website in the byline of the article so people know who you are, that you're a public speaker, and how to reach you. You'd be surprised at how many author bylines don't include the word "speaker." How am I supposed to know you speak, if you don't refer to yourself as a speaker?

Where should you submit articles for publication? To whatever website is most relevant for your subject matter. If you speak about cats (I'm sure someone out there is making money speaking about cats), then write for ilovecats.com. If you speak about mindfulness, then write for Mind Body Green and other popular wellness websites. The website Contently maintains a great list of different publications and the rates they pay freelance writers (newsflash: most publications don't pay their writers very well). Here's a breakdown of several websites where speakers in the business world should submit content on a frequent basis:

**Your own blog**
Pros: It's your blog, so you can write whatever you want. Good to build a connection with your followers.
Cons: The only people who read your blog are going to be your followers—it's hard to bring other readers to your site.

## Medium

Pros: Anyone can post on Medium, and you can submit to topic-focused publications which helps with cultivating new followers. You also retain the rights to your work so you can re-post elsewhere. Check out the list of top publications on Medium for where to submit.

Cons: Since anyone can post on Medium, people might not take your work as seriously as if it were published by a formal publication.

## LinkedIn

Pros: Anyone can post on LinkedIn. There are lots of readers working in the HR/sales/corporate arena, so it's good for lead generation. People may view your LinkedIn profile after reading your articles, which is a plus.

Cons: Since anyone can post on LinkedIn, it's hard to make your work stand out.

## Huffington Post

Pros: It's pretty easy to start writing for them—you just need to know someone that already writes for Huffington Post to make an intro for you. There is potential to go viral if you write a timely post with a headline that's clickbait-y.

Cons: HuffPo is unpaid, over-saturated, and not very well-respected. Most content does not go viral and only gets read by the people you share it with.

**Forbes** (also check out *Inc.* and *Entrepreneur*)

Pros: The brand has a strong reputation, and many people take *Forbes* seriously. There's potential for a large readership through *Forbes'* popular social media channels.

Cons: Increasingly, a lot of *Forbes* articles read like press releases for the people or companies they are covering.

**Fast Company** (also check out *Business Insider*, *Quartz*, *Mic.*, *VICE*, etc.)

Pros: Respected and read by many in the tech and business world.

Cons: Many article submissions are rejected by the editors; there's usually a higher bar for quality submissions than *Forbes*.

**Harvard Business Review**

Pros: Highly-respected, *HBR* is the Holy Grail of business publications. If you write for *HBR*, people assume you're an expert and will likely want to book you for speaking or consulting.

Cons: It's harder to get the green light on your submission, unless you are highly connected or have a proven track record of accomplishment.

# Exercise: Get cited as an expert

In addition to writing guest posts, a great way to get speaking leads is to get cited as an expert in other writer's articles. Have you ever noticed in publications like *Fast Company*, *Forbes*, and *Inc.*, how they always cite experts? "Adam Smiley Poswolsky, millennial workplace expert and author of *The Quarter-Life Breakthrough*, says avocado toast is definitely here to stay..." For this exercise, I challenge you to get cited as an expert in at least one article in the next month. There are several simple ways to make this happen. First, sign-up for websites like HARO (Help a Reporter Out), where you list your areas of expertise and contact info, and journalists can reach out to you for quotes. Second, reach out to writers in your area of expertise via Twitter or email, letting them know you are available for comment or interview. Third, add a media kit or press page to your website, so folks know where you've been featured.

# 24

# Why standing in your truth matters

**HERE'S A STORY ABOUT** what can happen when you start sharing what's on your mind. My friend Saya Iwasaki is a talented graphic designer, educator, and empowerment designer. She got her master's degree from Stanford University Graduate School of Education, and has worked with IDEO U, EdSurge, One Workplace, Nasdaq Entrepreneurship Center, and helped manage an innovative school in Myanmar. Over the past year or so, she became more and more interested in the blockchain and cryptocurrency space, noticing that most of the blockchain ecosystem was dominated by the wealthy, and that diversity was seriously lacking among blockchain leaders (and speakers).

Saya put pen to paper and drafted a popular Medium article titled, "Blockchain is a '1%' Conversation, and That Needs to Change," advocating for empowering the voices of more women, people of color, and international communities in the blockchain space. The piece was published by the popular Medium publication HackerNoon and was shared around the Internet. "It was the most opinionated piece I've ever written," Saya told me. "I was scared to write it, and some of the first comments attacked me. But I learned that you have to be willing to go to bat for your beliefs. If no one else is talking about it, and you're thinking it, then your voice matters."

Overcoming her fears paid off. Saya's post led to speaking opportunities about blockchain at General Assembly, SAP, and an industrial design conference. She spoke at a Women in Blockchain meetup, led a Block-chain 101 workshop, was interviewed by *Forbes* Japan, and was hired for contract work with a famous professional athlete who's passionate about increasing diversity in the blockchain ecosystem. Perhaps most exciting of all, the post even led to a full-time job working with a blockchain startup called Bitski, which builds tools supporting accessibility in the blockchain space.

Sharing your truth isn't just about booking a speaking gig and making a few bucks. It's about putting your ideas out there—especially the ideas that no one else is talking about that matter the most. Raising your voice just might lead to a new job offer, or even a new career path. Raising your voice will allow you to connect with others to help build your dreams.

## 25

# How I made $10,000 from writing an article for free

**IF YOU THINK IT'S ANNOYING** that some events don't pay speakers, talk to a few writers. Writing is another industry that consistently asks people to work for free in exchange for exposure and other career opportunities. Much of the online content you read on *Huffington Post*, *Forbes*, *Fast Company*, *Business Insider*, or *Inc.*, to name a few, was written for free by a contributor looking to build their personal brand.

On the one hand, this is wack. No one should work for free and it pains me that these multi-million dollar media companies are profiting from advertising money due to my friends' unpaid labor. On the other hand, I've written dozens of articles that I've never been paid for, but that I've used as leverage for my career. In 2014, I wrote a piece for *Fast Company* about millennial entrepreneurship for free. Someone who worked at the global tech company SAP (which has an annual revenue of $22 billion and employs 84,000 people in 180 countries) loved the piece and asked if I would be willing to join SAP's annual conference, SAP Sapphire in Orlando, Florida, to speak on a panel. The gig was unpaid, but SAP agreed to cover my travel and lodging.

One year later, in 2015, the same employee at SAP recommended me to speak at SAP Sapphire again, but this time I gave a keynote and was paid $10,000, plus travel and expenses. I've also done several other paid gigs with SAP over the years.

Was it worth writing the piece for *Fast Company* for free? I think so. Even if I had been paid to write it, *Fast Company* probably pays about $150-200 an article, which is ridiculous given that it took me two weeks to write (that's like $3 an hour). Are the publications screwing you? Sure. But you can make them work for you while you're getting screwed. This is why it's important to write relevant content about your Speaker Zone of Genius, Anchor, Hook, and Pain Point.

# 26

# Write a book that matters

**WRITING A BOOK IS THE MOST** popular anchor used to break into the speaking industry. As you've probably gathered from my story, my book definitely was a competitive advantage to help establish credibility, authority, and position me as a millennial expert. Corporations *love* authors. If you were an event planner deciding between two speakers, and one of them had written a popular book and the other hadn't, which speaker would you go with?

I highly recommend you write a book if you want to grow your speaking business. My writing journey included initially self-publishing *The Quarter-Life Breakthrough*, getting a $50,000 book deal with TarcherPerigee/Penguin Random House to re-write *The Quarter-Life Breakthrough*, and then self-publishing this book after it was rejected by publishers. Here are a few things I learned along the way:

1.  **Write a book because you have a story that needs to be told, not because you want to make money.**

This one should be obvious for anyone who writes for a living, but writing may not lead to much income. A $50,000 advance might sound like a lot of money, but that's before taxes, my agent's fee, and when you break that money down over the four years it took me to write my book, writing is far less lucrative than working at a coffee shop. I started writing because I knew others were facing the same questions I was, and that my story could help them. Whenever I get emails from readers telling me that reading my book inspired them to re-think what they wanted to do with their life, it makes all the time I spent writing worth it.

2. **Whether you self-publish or publish, you are going to do a shit-ton of work.**
   If you're hella famous, you can either publish or self-publish and you'll be good. Newsflash: famous people are pretty much always going to be fine. If you're not famous (like I was in 2013), I think the way to go is self-publishing since you don't really have a choice anyway. Not-famous people don't usually get book deals. The people who usually get book deals have a very large platform and have accomplished something pretty remarkable.

   Self-publishing offers an incredible opportunity to share your ideas with the world. I've been inspired by what author James Altucher calls "Publishing 3.0" and Guy Kawasaki's theory that a writer is an author, publisher, and entrepreneur. Your book will be as good as you make it, regardless of whether it's being published by Penguin Random House or yourself. Writing a book is just the beginning. The real work is getting it out to the world. Over the past four years, I have done everything for my book; from writing blog posts to making a video trailer to hosting events to spending hours at the post office, mailing copies of the book to journalists. Writing a book is like running your own start-up venture.

3. **Being an author is not really about writing; it's about connecting with your readers.**
   Book marketing expert Tim Grahl stresses the importance of creating a system where you continue to connect with your readers through your email list and your platform, where you can share interesting content and build community. Marketing a book doesn't start with your book launch, it starts with building an audience (which often takes a year, or many years) before you even decide to write a book. A successful book requires successful long-term community engagement, which means your book is not about you, it's about the people who care about you and what you're writing about.

4. **For the purpose of booking speaking engagements, how your book is perceived is your calling card.**

Obviously, you should put time into your marketing plan and you should aim to sell as many books as possible. But, I am living proof that you don't need to sell hundreds of thousands of books to get a lot of speaking engagements. Writing a really good book (that is received well by experts in your industry, gains a bunch of press mentions, and has a lot of positive Amazon reviews) is far more important than how many books you sell. I've sold more than 10,000 copies of *The Quarter-Life Breakthrough* (between the first two editions). 10,000 books is a solid number of books—most self-published books barely sell 100 copies and most published books barely sell 1000 copies—but it's still not that many books. Big-name authors sometimes sell 10,000 books in a week. I haven't earned much money from selling books the past few years. However, I've earned over $100,000 a year of speaking revenue during the time I've been a published author.

The important thing is to write a book that matters, one that establishes your authority in your niche and anchors your speaking career. Your job is to write a really good book that becomes your calling card for speaking gigs (as well as for other ventures like consulting, coaching, courses, full-time and part-time job opportunities, etc.). And hey, if your book sells hundreds of thousands of copies while you're at it, awesome. You can buy me a kombucha.

# 27

# Stand out: make your content fresh and exciting

**EARLIER, I WROTE ABOUT** the importance of practicing one talk over and over again, until you become a one-hit wonder. This process can be creatively draining and boring. As you progress in your speaking career, it's important to keep exploring new mediums and find ways to create fresh content, even as you carve your niche within a niche.

My friend Sarah K Peck is a writer, startup advisor, and communications expert, and is currently writing a book called *Startup Pregnant*, about her experience in the tech world while pregnant. In order to build her audience (and practice her speaking), she's been hosting a weekly podcast called The Startup Pregnant Podcast featuring stories of women in leadership, life, and parenting. The podcast has become incredibly popular, hitting 30,000 downloads within the first six months, and doubling its reach every month.

Another speaker friend of mine, John Henry, creates short and informative 20-second videos on Instagram (where he has 40,000 followers) and hosts a series on YouTube called Uptown Hustle. John is a Dominican-American serial entrepreneur, investor, and public speaker based in Harlem. He started his first company at 18. He now serves as a Managing Partner at Harlem Capital Partners, an impact investment firm focused on finding the next generation of great, diverse entrepreneurs. These simple but well-produced videos allow John to test out new material for his talks, and demonstrate his speaking expertise to the world.

Goldie Chan is a digital marketing expert and keynote speaker, and a top LinkedIn video creator, with over 2.5 million content views. Goldie has built up a huge following on LinkedIn by producing short, engaging videos for the site. When was the last time you heard someone say they were focused on building a huge LinkedIn following? Probably never, because everyone thinks Instagram is 500 times cooler than LinkedIn. That's exactly why Goldie's content stands out on the site—and why she has over 25,000 followers. Her videos about social media, personal branding, and general lifestyle advice are far more interesting than the majority of boring business and sales posts by boring old white dudes that appear on LinkedIn every day. Her voice is friendly, approachable, and very refreshing—and she's got neon green hair! Goldie did a one-minute video interviewing me about my three tips to become a top paid speaker, and it was viewed over 15,000 times. In short, Goldie makes LinkedIn cool again (actually, let's be real here, has LinkedIn ever been cool?). Her work has been featured in *Forbes*, *Inc.*, and *Fast Company*, and Goldie recently built an online course with LinkedIn Learning about how to produce effective video content.

My buddy Max Stossel is a storyteller, poet, film-maker, and digital activist. Combining these fields, Max creates beautifully produced videos featuring his spoken word poems with digital effects. His video called "Stop Making Murderers Famous" questions why the media gives so much screen time to the perpetrators of mass shootings, instead of telling the victims' stories. It reached five million views on Facebook alone in a week. Another video called "This Panda Is Dancing" was launched with Time Well Spent, a movement to align our technology with our humanity, and explores how our phones and apps manipulate our attention and keep us from spending time in-person with the people we care about most. It also was viewed over one million times. Max's work has won two Webby awards, and he frequently speaks at companies, colleges, and events.

Maybe the medium is short videos, or a podcast, or blogging, or hosting live events, or sharing your art. The point is: start exploring new media to keep your work fresh and exciting.

## Exercise: Brave new content

In the next month, create a piece of content that is completely different from your previous work. If you've never written an article on Medium before, write an article on Medium. If you've never recorded an Instagram video before, record an Instagram video. If you've never been on a podcast before, find a podcast to be on (or record your own podcast episode using Skype or YouTube!). If you've never uploaded a slide deck to SlideShare, upload a slide deck. If you've already done all these things, I challenge you to create a piece of content in a medium you've never previously explored.

# Interview with Tim Mousseau

"Specialize, specialize, specialize."

Tim Mousseau is a top speaker with CAMPUSPEAK, a college speaking agency, and for the first three years of his speaking career, he worked full-time at Buhv Designs in Denver, Colorado. Tim speaks to universities, colleges, and nonprofits about sexual violence prevention, masculinity, and leadership. He has been a speaker for four years, done over 170 speaking engagements, and been paid to speak over 150 times, reaching some 125,000 college students.

## Why did you start public speaking?

In graduate school, I quickly became enamored with the power of sharing my ideas. At the time, I was studying organizational leadership and wanted to become the next Simon Sinek. As time went on, I loved the aspect of speaking but as I began writing more, I found myself questioning whether my general leadership keynotes were creating actual change. A shift in thinking led me to focusing on the subject of speaking about sexual violence prevention from the role of a male survivor of sexual assault. I speak in order to de-stigmatize the field of sexual violence and make as much of a change as possible for other survivors, to change how organizations are discussing sexual violence, and to prevent this crime from occurring.

**How did you get your first speaking gig? How did it go?**

My first speaking gig happened while I was working for a higher-ed based nonprofit in Indianapolis. Rutgers University sponsored me to come to their campus and speak to student leaders about leaving an impact. It went awful. I had never done a full, hour-long keynote before and my timing was entirely off. The stories didn't flow well together and the end result was a highly checked out audience. The only benefit of this program lay in reframing how I viewed speaking in general and my responsibilities to my audience.

**Over time, how have you made your keynote better and better? How do you test material?**

I always carry around a notebook in my pocket, and after every keynote I create two lists. The first list is things that went well and the second is things that did not. I try to be extremely specific in remembering items for each category, and I always jot down a minimum of three. I use this to decipher what might be working, what needs fixing, and what might be situational. For example, if an item constantly shows up on my positive list and shows up only once on the negative list, the poor reaction could be based on the crowd or general atmosphere. If something is constantly showing up on my negative list at least two to three times, I will update accordingly.

I test new ideas slowly. First, I will practice them on my own to measure out the pacing, emphasis, and ensure I am comfortable adopting them into my work. From there, I will only ever make one major change to a keynote at a time. I am always cautious to change too much at once because then I am unsure whether or not the keynote might not be working due to the content or my lack of familiarity.

**What is the primary thing that separates speakers who get booked a lot from speakers who don't?**

Specialize, specialize, specialize. I get infinitely more bookings coming from my unique lens as a male survivor of sexual violence and industry recognized expert than I do from my MA research on leadership. People want you to be able to provide a unique value they can get from no one else or at least a limited pool of competitors. The more general you are, or the more you talk on general ideas, the worse. And you have to offer value. People book because somehow, some way, you are creating change or impacting their bottom line or meeting a metric they have set for success.

**What's the difference between an engaging keynote and a boring one?**

An engaging keynote meets the audience where they are while still challenging them. Speak to the knowledge level of your primary base and never treat them as uneducated but understand you are bringing them new ideas and illuminating content for them. Engaging keynotes are not just about the speaker or their ego but pull from a variety of sources for stories. Also, stories should not just be cliché or handed down maxims taken from others. Lastly, 70/30 rule. 70 percent engagement and 30 percent education. With the amount of content existing in the world, keynotes have increasingly become about how you make an audience feel versus what you teach them.

**What would be your advice for a new speaker trying to break into the college speaking market?**

As with any industry but especially within higher education, it is about knowing the language, policies, and needs of your audiences. You must be able to speak to the students directly while addressing the concerns and needs of the campus professionals. Language is a big deal in higher education and if you cannot speak it properly or do not know how to interface with your contacts, it can damage a relationship and your potential long-term options.

**Connect with Tim:** timmousseau.com,
Twitter: @TimMousseau, Instagram: tim_mousseau

# 28

# The audience is your classroom

**WHEN I FIRST STARTED SPEAKING,** I was too nervous to sit through other speakers' talks. I wanted to focus on doing a great job with my presentation, so I'd spend most conferences chilling in my hotel room or nervously pacing back and forth outside the venue. Now I realize I was missing out on a huge opportunity: the chance to see other speakers in action. Watching other speakers teaches you what works and what doesn't. In *TED Talks*, Chris Anderson shares how one time a TED speaker spent most of his talk going on and on about how great his own consulting services were, until Chris had to interrupt the speaker and ask him to share something valuable. The experience was excruciating but I bet no one that was sitting in that audience has ever again given a speech about how great their business is.

When you sit in the audience during other presentations, pay attention to what makes you smile, what leaves you wanting more, and what makes you cringe.

Personally, I hate it when speakers look at their phones or iPads during a talk. Even if they're looking at notes, it comes off as rude and distracting, because there's still the possibility that they are actually checking Instagram or Tinder while they're on stage. So, the next time you watch another speaker, take notes. What are they doing that you don't like? What are they doing that seems really effective? Is there anything from their talk you can incorporate in your own?

The conferences you don't speak at are just as important as the ones you *do* speak at. Make a list of all the conferences in your field and check out who's being booked to speak. Get to know the ecosystem of speakers in your niche. Study those speakers' websites. Even more importantly, study the titles and descriptions of the sessions they are offering. Is the title of their talk more compelling than yours? If so, why? What language are they using to describe their presentation? What can you learn from similar speakers in your subject area?

# Exercise: Study similar speakers

When you're submitting a book proposal to get a book deal from a publisher, the publisher asks you to list competitive titles that are similar to your book. Many authors assume the publisher wants to hear, "No book has ever been written about this subject, I'm the first!" But the truth is that the publisher wants to know that the author has a deep understanding of the competitive landscape for their book. This knowledge applies to speaking as well.

Make a list of 4-5 speakers who are your top competitors. Not the most famous speakers in the world, but speakers who are often booked to speak about a similar topic that you speak about. If you aren't sure who your competition is, do a Google search for speakers about your topic, and check out the speakers who appear on the first page of the search results. Now, study those speakers' websites, reels, program descriptions, past speaking appearances, and marketing assets. What's different? What do you like about their work? What do you prefer about your own work? What can you learn from these speakers? What can you do differently to separate yourself from the competition?

# 29

# Your program description matters

**IN ADDITION TO COMING UP** with a catchy title for your presentation, it's worth spending time on your talk description. Usually, conferences will ask you to submit a 1-paragraph description of your session, either with your application or after you've already been asked to speak. This means that they're reading the conference description to determine whether your subject matter is interesting for your audience. The description thus becomes part of the sales process. With a good description, you book the gig; with a boring one, they choose another speaker. I recommend keeping these conference descriptions as brief and simple as possible: 3-4 sentences that outline your overall argument and a few key points you'll be making.

Here's a description for my program on "Building a Purpose-Driven Career," which is for college students:

As an author and speaker, Smiley inspires students to have quarter-life breakthroughs, find meaningful work, and change the world. In Building a Purpose-Driven Career, Smiley offers inspiring lessons for young people to build careers on meaning, not money. He talks about the importance of surrounding yourself with believers, asking for what you want, discovering what's meaningful to you, building a healthy relationship with social media, building a supportive network of advisors and mentors, and how to hustle with intention to achieve your goals.

Here's a description for my keynote on "Creating a Purpose-Driven Workplace: How to Attract, Retain, and Empower Millennial Talent," which is for companies and conferences.

Despite struggling with debt, recession, and the jobs crisis, millennials (who already account for the majority of the workforce) are not motivated by money. Rather, they are driven to make the world more compassionate, innovative, and sustainable. During this interactive session, we'll learn how meaning-hungry millennials are reshaping the future of work, as well as practical tools for attracting, retaining and empowering top talent, and strategies to foster intergenerational collaboration that will help you build a purpose-driven workplace that engages all your employees.

Stay away from jargon and as they tell you in journalism, "Don't bury the lede." Get to the point and tell people what your keynote is about. Pro tip: keep the program guides and bookmark websites for conferences you go to, then highlight the descriptions that are most exciting to you. How can you make your own session title and program description better?

## Exercise: Brainstorm a new program description

It's hard to write the perfect program description. One description might work for some conferences or companies, but not for others. To maximize the number of gigs you book, it's best to write three different program descriptions for each of your talks. Yes, the talk title might be the same each time, and the talk itself might be the same, but the *language you use to describe the talk* is different. If you're stuck on writing three different descriptions, try this: write one "serious" description using information and statistics, one "provocative" description that catches the reader's eye by being controversial or thought-provoking, and one "fun" description that uses humor or satire.

# 30

# Cater your message to different audiences

**JUST BECAUSE YOU'RE PASSIONATE** about a topic doesn't mean your audience will care. I learned this through practice. When I first started speaking, the majority of my talks were for college students and unemployed young professionals figuring out the next step in their career. I learned that colleges weren't an ideal customer base for me, because often they had their own career centers and were already spending tons of resources on career counseling services and career advisors for students. In short, many colleges felt like they didn't need to bring in an outside expert to help their students find a job and navigate life after college. I disagree with this assumption, but that's their decision to make.

I also found out that 20-somethings who were looking for a job responded to my message well, but didn't make ideal customers either, because they were unemployed and usually broke (after all, the average college student these days is graduating with \$30,000 of student debt), so these talks were almost always unpaid.

I also learned pretty quickly—and not surprisingly—that companies *did not* want me to tell their employees to quit their job. It took me about twenty speaking engagements to realize that the best fit for my message was actually companies, specifically HR and talent teams, wanting to learn how best to hire, retain, and engage the next generation of talent. Even though I wrote a book about the quarter-life crisis, my talks became much more about millennials in the workplace, the future of work, employee engagement, intergenerational collaboration, and how to build a purpose-driven company culture. In business, this is called product/market fit. You have to figure out the best audience for your product, and it might be different than what you initially think it's going to be.

These days, I have different keynotes I deliver to college students, young professionals, and executives at companies. The keynotes share a common message around meaningful work, but they are different because I've learned that these audiences want different things. One way to craft different keynotes is to use what's referred to as the "sandwich approach"—I'm not sure who came up with it, but it's a useful analogy.

Once you have your core opening and closing of your talk fleshed out (the bread of your sandwich), you can begin playing with different material in the middle (changing what type of toppings you're putting inside the sandwich), based on the audience. As you gain more experience on stage, try making subtle shifts to your core message and testing new material, new slides, and even a new opening or closing every now and then. Instead of coming up with a new talk every time you go on stage, you can riff off your one-hit wonder and make incremental changes and improvements every gig.

# 31

# How to have a successful sales call with a meeting planner or conference organizer

**WHEN AN EVENT PLANNER** or conference organizer reaches out to you, expressing interest in having you speak at their event, they often have not finalized their roster of speakers. Thus, the call you have with them so they can "learn more about your work and see whether you'd be a good fit" is a crucial sales call: it's your opportunity to prove to the organizer that they should book you and not someone else. Here are a few things you want to make sure you do on these calls:

1. **Be prepared.** Do background research about the company or event ahead of time. Know who else is

speaking there, or who they booked to speak the previous year.

2. **Ask questions.** This is the perfect chance to learn more about the audience you'll be addressing and the key problems they are struggling with.

3. **Demonstrate why they should pick you.** Detail how will you add value for the audience. Perhaps you recently spoke to a similar group? Maybe you just wrote an article about the topic?

4. **Authentically connect.** Being curious, excited, and giving the meeting planner a few (honest) compliments about their event or the work they're doing, never hurts. If a planner asks if you can change a few parts of your presentation to meet their needs, your answer should be, "Of course I can!" Figure out how to make meeting planners happy and you'll always have gigs waiting for you.

What happens when an event organizer is a little 'too involved' in your presentation? You'll occasionally come across planners who want to see three drafts of your talk, and maybe even do a full run-through on the phone before the conference. There's nothing more annoying for a speaker than a planner that wants to micro-manage your talk. In my opinion, a good organizer should book a good speaker and then let that speaker do their job. However, if you're working with an organizer that's a little too hands-on, always be respectful, but stand up for yourself, too. Answer their questions, address their concerns, send them any additional links as needed, but also remind them of your experience and professionalism. Sometimes you have to work a little harder to earn their trust, but it'll be worth it when you do.

## Exercise: Do your homework

I have Google Alerts set-up for "millennials," "millennials in the workplace," "future of work," and "meaningful work." This means that whenever there's a relevant article for my work, I get an email notification. Now, to be honest, I don't read most of these articles since there are dozens every day, but I do review the ones that seem especially relevant. Reading relevant articles and research is where I find new material to add to my talks. A good talk should incorporate a few statistics and a relevant study or two, so stay on top of the trends in your industry.

Bonus tip: new studies and research can be great prompts for you to write thought leadership pieces in relevant blogs and websites, which can help you get discovered for speaking gigs. Lead generation starts with doing your homework. Set up Google Alerts for a few keywords related to your talk. Commit to reading 2-3 new articles each week about your subject.

## 32

# Keep your panel from sucking

**IN A RECENT BLOG POST CALLED** "Why Panels Suck," LinkedIn founder and CEO Reid Hoffman writes, "At thousands of conferences every year, millions of panel sessions consume billions of man-hours of attention. And for what? A panel is an algorithm that makes three to six leaders in a given field sound dull." While every single conference is full of dozens of panels, the truth is that Reid Hoffman is right: most panels are pretty boring. It's hard to engage in a true debate or interesting conversation when you have more than four people on stage. Furthermore, panels leave audience members out of the equation and often turn into opportunities for the panelists to brag about how great they are.

If you do find yourself organizing, moderating, or sitting on a panel, here are few simple things to remember to keep your panel from sucking.

1. **Keep it small.** Never have more than four people (including the moderator) on a panel, otherwise you'll have too many people for an intimate conversation.

2. **Make it diverse.** There is nothing worse than the BOWD-el (that's a panel of six Boring Old White Dudes), or a MAN-el, or any panel that is only representing one type of person. The most interesting panels I've organized have included a variety of folks coming to a particular topic from different backgrounds, organizations, and perspectives.

3. **Keep intros to 30-seconds.** The moderator must keep the panelists from spending 5-minutes introducing themselves, otherwise time will be up before you've even discussed anything interesting.

4. **Trade talking points for personal stories.** The key to an exciting panel is getting your panelists to go off-script. This happens when the moderator is prepared and asks deeply personal questions. The more you get your panelists to tell their own stories, instead of talking about how great their company is, the more your audience will be engaged.

5. **Open it up to audience Q&A early.** There's also nothing worse than watching a panel and hearing the moderator say, "I'm so sorry, we've run out of time for questions,

have a great day!" This is an indication of a shitty panel moderator. Q&A is the most interesting part of a panel for the audience. Make sure you leave at least 10 minutes—preferably 15 minutes—for audience questions.

# 33

# Make it interactive

**THE FUTURE OF PUBLIC SPEAKING** is not panels (or keynote presentations), it's interactive conversations and workshops that emphasize audience participation and experience over the speaker's accomplishments. With the proliferation of TED talks and online video, it's become easier and easier to watch a keynote speaker give their talk from the comfort of your home computer screen or your iPhone. So why the hell would you want to pay them to give the *same exact talk* with the *same exact slides* at your office, company retreat, or conference stage?

What does this mean for speakers? It means the traditional keynote talk and the six-person BOWD-el as we know it is a thing of the past. On the one hand, this means we get rid of a lot of Boring Old White Dudes! Awesome. Good riddance. Most of them didn't belong on stage anyway.

On the other hand, it means that keynote speakers like you and me, who actually aren't boring, but basically still just deliver a standard keynote from the stage with a PowerPoint presentation will need to find ways to make their material more interesting. It means all speakers will need to provide more time for audience interaction and participation.

It's scary for me to say this, since I make a living from delivering keynote presentations, but I expect there to be less and less keynotes booked in the next five years. The keynote talk is old school. One person with a slide clicker standing in front of a room, and a bunch of people sitting in rows listening? *Borrrring.* No wonder most people are on their phones (or snoozing) during conferences.

It's amazing that the events industry hasn't been disrupted sooner. In the future, event organizers will be booking speakers who can give engaging fireside chats where they are interviewed on-the-spot by a moderator, speakers who can debate their topics with someone who holds a different view than them, and most importantly: *speakers who can deliver a presentation that takes audience members through a participatory and transformational journey.*

This is already happening in the college market, and starting to become more popular in the corporate market as well. My friend Jordan Axani runs a speakers bureau called Shift Collaboration, that delivers interactive workshops for college and high school students. If you want to predict the future, pay attention to what millennial and Gen-Z markets are demanding. In his mental health program called "What's Your Big Lie," Jordan uses mobile technology to allow students to share their most painful life experiences anonymously and safely. His team sets up stations around campus where students can participate in the hours leading up to the presentation. The presentation itself is focused on audience sharing and participation, to make students realize that they are not alone when it comes to struggling with anxiety, depression, and mental health challenges.

Rates of depression among Gen-Z, the so-called Smartphone Generation, are soaring. Professor of Psychology Jean Twenge from San Diego State University notes that between 2010 and 2015, the number of U.S. teens who felt useless and joyless (which are classic symptoms of depression) surged by 33 percent. Teen suicide attempts increased 23 percent, and the number of 13- to 18-year-olds who committed suicide jumped 31 percent. Many researchers believe that digital devices and young people's relationship to social media are a big part of the problem.

Another talented speaker I know, Larissa May, who is only 24, speaks on college campuses and leads in-person workshops on the intersection of social media and well-being. Larissa is the founder of Half the Story, which reminds people that behind the beautiful photos and 'everything is awesome' captions on Instagram, things are not as rosy as they might seem. Half the Story's Instagram account (which has nearly 20,000 followers) tries to make social media a place where people can discuss intimate topics like depression, anxiety, envy, and low self-esteem. Half the Story was recently named one of CNN's "7 startups that want to improve your mental health," and Larissa's work has been featured in *Forbes*, *Health*, *TIME*, ABC's Good Morning America, Now This, and Girlboss.

Another friend of mine, Adam Rosendahl, delivers an engaging program called LATE NITE ART. Instead of merely talking about art, he leads participants on a two-hour creative journey full of painting, drawing, live music, play, dance, intimate conversation, and personal growth. LATE NITE ART is incredibly popular at conferences and companies because it's fun, and infinitely more interesting than watching someone talk about how cool their start-up is.

Tom Chi is one of the pioneers of rapid prototyping in tech, and the most brilliant person I know. He used to be the head of experience at GoogleX, and helped design the prototype for the Google Glass with his colleagues, using a coat hanger and sheet protector that fourth graders use for book reports. How long did the prototype take to build? One day—actually, only forty-five minutes. Tom has also worked in senior roles at Yahoo and Microsoft and as a mentor for The Unreasonable Institute. When Tom gives a talk, he doesn't just talk about rapid prototyping, he facilitates a rapid prototyping exercise. Audience members are given construction paper, clay, pipe cleaners, aluminum foil, cardboard boxes, and other crafts, to create physical prototypes in small groups. The participants then go through the experience of getting live feedback and incorporating user experience on their product prototypes, which is the essential lesson of Tom's presentation: the most effective way to learn and solve problems is by doing. In his words, "how can you maximize the rate of learning by minimizing the rate of time to try ideas?"

I've seen Tom's talk eleven different times. Seriously, eleven times? Yes, eleven times. Maybe even twelve. Even though Tom's talk is essentially the same each time, it never feels repetitive or boring. First off, Tom is a genius. But really, this is because the bulk of his presentation relies on a participatory exercise with the audience members, so it's always fresh because each audience becomes *part of the presentation*. Each talk is different because the audience is learning new ideas and creating new projects as part of the talk.

I once saw my friend Torin Perez make an audience feel comfortable, engaged, and seen within the first 30 seconds of his presentation. Torin speaks about inclusive leadership and authentic storytelling, was a member of the inaugural TED Residency, and is the author of *Who Am I to Lead?*, a collection of short essays that embolden us to embrace our whole selves while leading positive change. I asked Torin what his secrets were to engaging audiences. "Believe it or not, I do this before I even get on stage," he shared.

**"I use the power of visualization to see myself succeeding in engaging my audience. I vividly picture the reactions,**

smiles, laughter, and a-ha moments before they even happen. When I stand in front of the people I'm about to speak to, I just live what I've already seen and do my best to create an incredible experience each person will never forget... I challenge myself to try different styles of interacting with my audiences, from having no slides, to incorporating music and dance, to 1:1 paired activities, small groups, and full group participation in repeating something I've said. If you believe that the exercise has value and people should do it, try it out! You wouldn't believe how many audiences I've gotten to dance."

Regardless of your topic, start thinking about ways to make your talk more interactive and audience-forward. Your speaking career might depend on it.

# Exercise: Make it interactive

How can you take material you normally share in a keynote and make it more participatory? Brainstorm a 5-10 minute activity that fits in your talk for each of the following scenarios:

1. Individual reflection
2. Partner share (1-on-1)
3. Small group activity (3-5 people)
4. Entire room activity

At your next speaking engagement, try incorporating at least one of these interactive activities into your talk.

# 34

# Make it Personal

**EARLIER, I MENTIONED** the work Ashanti Branch is doing to improve the emotional well-being of underserved and at-risk young men of color. When Ashanti was a dean at his former high school, Fremont High School in California, he realized that a lot of the boys and teenagers he was working with were saying everything in their lives was going fine, while in reality, things were much darker. Ashanti wanted to find a way for the students to get vulnerable and share what they were actually dealing with—he wanted them to be able to take off the masks they were wearing.

Ashanti developed an interactive exercise where his students could draw the emotions they presented to the outside world (their 'masks'), and then draw what was actually beneath the mask. When participants started sharing what was underneath, they shared common feelings of pain, loss, lack of self-worth, lack of love, fear, loneliness, anxiety, depression, and anger.

"When people go through the second part of the workshop, they get a chance to talk about the things that nobody would ever know by looking at them," Ashanti explains. "When you can hear others express who they really are, and then you have an option in return to express who you really are—versus continuing with the mask—it's an opportunity to open up, and many people don't get that opportunity ever!"

Ashanti's workshop isn't only for teenagers; it's just as powerful for adults. I've participated in Ashanti's workshop five times: with entrepreneurs, corporate executives, and accomplished leaders from around the world, and every single time, the audience is in tears by the end of the presentation. This is because Ashanti is a highly-skilled facilitator who creates a safe space for participants to open up, be vulnerable, and in his words, "express who they really are." The more your workshop or presentation allows your audience to get personal with themselves and each other, the more transformational it will be.

My friend Shira Abramowitz, the director of programming at Summit, who has helped curate over 1,000 speakers for more than 150 Summit events, offers another useful framing for making your talks more personal. Shira says, "While it can be appealing to stand up on a stage and command attention, a better question for a speaker is, what can you do to bring yourself to eye level with the audience? How can you break down the power dynamics such that you're actually in it together, and they see you not as an iconic speaker, but rather as a friend?"

How can you get your audience out of their head and into their body, or as Ashanti puts it, into their heart?

# 35

# Prepare for the future of conferences and experience design

**FOR THE SAME REASON** that the keynote presentation is increasingly being replaced by the interactive workshop, the entire meetings industry itself is headed for a major reinvention. The conference of the future will be small, intimate, and emphasize the participant experience over who is on the main stage.

I recently spoke at The Culture Conference, an invite-only summit designed for leaders in employee engagement, learning and development, HR and talent operations, diversity and inclusion, and corporate culture. The Culture Conference was directed by Jenny Sauer-Klein, co-founder of AcroYoga and founder of Play on Purpose, with the mission of answering the question: how can we transform leaders, teams and organizational culture from the inside out? Jenny's business focuses on designing experiences that are engaging and interactive, and the art of facilitating those experiences. She helps speakers become better facilitators, and helps event designers design more experiential events.

One of Jenny's primary goals with The Culture Conference was to create a new paradigm of conference, one that emphasized the participant experience. If you go to lots of conferences like I do, you've also probably grown weary of huge hotel ballrooms, too many keynote speakers, complicated apps that nobody ends up using, endless rows of chairs, awful hotel buffet food, and not enough time for in-person interaction. If you went to a business conference ten years ago, you could probably hear everyone at the local Hilton be like, "Lord, kill me now. Get me out of here. Why did I come to this awful conference?"

In contrast, the business conferences of the next decade are going to be as fun as going on a weekend getaway with your friends. Conferences are becoming curated, highly experiential events. The rooms you speak in will be smaller, chairs will no longer be in rows, events will source delicious and nutritious food (think food trucks and locally-inspired food, not gross hotel buffets), be hosted at unique venues instead of cookie-cutter hotels (think a camp in the woods or a beautiful retreat center, not the Hilton), offer time for play, dance, wellness, and nature activities, and be more intentional about creating a comfortable and memorable experience for their attendees.

My friends at The Go Game speak at conferences and companies about the importance of playing like it's your job. But they don't just talk about play. They get people to play. At a Go Game program, participants play competitive team building games, which are designed to enhance communications, creativity, and problem-solving skills. Sometimes games involve participants competing in a scavenger hunt that takes them all around a venue or city.

Conferences are becoming fun, creative, exciting, and transformational because the millennial and Gen-Z markets are demanding them to be. I can't tell you how many millennial-focused events I go to where conference organizers want everyone to download a fancy app. Newsflash: young people don't fly thousands of miles and spend thousands of dollars to download an app or use a hashtag. They go to events to connect in-person with inspiring people, learn new ideas, and transform the way they live.

One study by Harris Group found that 78 percent of millennials prefer to spend more money on experiences than on material things, and that millennials are craving more experiences. Airbnb even launched a new product called Airbnb Experiences, to provide their customers with excursions and activities designed and led by local hosts, which grew twelve-fold in the first ten months of 2017 alone (thirteen times faster than Airbnb's homes business was growing at the same time). Airbnb earned about half a million dollars from their social impact experiences, and Brian Chesky, Airbnb's CEO, says the business is just starting to take off.

I recently attended EXP, an invite-only gathering in Napa Valley, California, which brought together 50 experience economy pioneers to learn from one another. The event was organized by Sarah Shewey, a co-founder and producer of TED Active and the founder and CEO of Happily. At EXP, I met organizers of experiential events like SXSW Interactive, TED, Daybreaker, Burning Man, and Woodstock. Breakfast was served in a 13th century Tuscan castle and another session took place in a natural mineral pool. Participants at EXP told me how refreshing it was to attend an event that provided ample time for attendees to connect with each other in small groups and 1-on-1.

People are tired of being herded from conference room to conference room and from keynote to keynote. The next generation is looking for events to provide fun and creative activities, personal and professional transformation, and breakthrough moments, not more screen time or more time sitting in a conference room. Public speakers, especially ones who are expert facilitators, team-builders, and community builders are going to be in even higher-demand in the transformative experience economy.

When I think of the best events I've attended, they all allow people to connect offline, and they create opportunities for "firsts": first times for people to overcome their fears, be creative, and find more clarity of purpose. The best events take the audience on an experiential and transformational journey. Recall the ancient proverb, "Tell me and I'll forget. Show me and I'll remember. Involve me and I'll understand." Your job is to *involve* the audience, to create a container for your audience to become a new person through the course of your presentation.

# PART III.
# GET PAID FOR
# YOUR TRUTH

# 36

# My trip (sadly, without Arya Stark) to Westeros to speak at King's Landing

**HERE'S A STORY ABOUT WHY** patience matters in the speaking business. After I self-published my book in 2014, I received an email from my friend Duleesha Kulasooriya, who worked at one of the largest consulting firms in the world. Duleesha and I met through mutual friends from Camp Grounded: Summer Camp for Adults. He had three adorable kids and worked at Deloitte, sported a mohawk and really colorful shirts, and went to Burning Man every year. I was like, *this dude is the coolest management consultant I've ever met.* Duleesha sent me an email connecting me to one of his colleagues.

Hey Adam,

**Wanted to connect you with one of our fellows, who would like to take point on seeing how we could help with your book launch. We have book clubs at Deloitte and have a national (even global) reach who we may be able to bring along to support your mission. Not to mention that they all love the topic!**

This email led me to doing book talks with junior fellows at Deloitte at their offices in San Francisco, Boston, New York, and Washington, D.C. Before I go on, I just want to clarify that Deloitte did not fly me to these places or pay me for these events. I was already going to be in these cities for my book tour, so I figured it would be worth meeting young Deloitte employees because they were my target audience. At each event, a few Deloitte fellows showed up, mostly for the free pizza Deloitte was offering, and I'd give a 15-minute spiel about my book and answer a few questions.

At the New York event, only four people showed up to listen to me! I was kind of embarrassed because I thought speaking at Deloitte was my big break. I figured I had made the big-time. I was even wearing the one suit I own for the gig. But even though only a few people showed up, and my talks were held in the cafeteria, I still gave the talks my best and signed books for folks who seemed interested.

Three years later, Duleesha hit me up with another email, this time asking if I wanted to speak about millennial engagement for Deloitte's Central European Partners Meeting in Dubrovnik, Croatia, all expenses paid, plus a speaking fee. Being a huge *Game of Thrones* fan, I knew that Dubrovnik's Old Town is where they shot a lot of the scenes for King's Landing and the Red Keep. I was like, "You want to fly me to King's Landing?! I mean, I was going to make the trek on horseback with Arya Stark, but sure, I'll fly business class instead."

This time, there were over 300 people in the audience and the stage looked like something out of a movie. I don't think I would have ever had the opportunity to speak in Croatia if I hadn't cultivated a relationship with my friend for over three years. Be patient. Booking corporate gigs takes time. Find the people within the corporation who are your champions. Don't be surprised if the first opportunity they offer you isn't a fancy one. After all, it took Daenerys eight seasons to make it to King's Landing, and she's the mother of dragons!

# 37

# Find the gatekeepers

**ONE OF THE REASONS** booking corporate speaking engagements is so difficult is that it's incredibly challenging to figure out who is in charge of selecting speakers for most organizations. I've never seen someone at a company with the job title: "Speaker Selector." There is no such person at most companies. I've been invited to speak by CEOs, VPs of talent, employees in HR departments, press officers, marketing associates, communications strategists, retreat planners, event coordinators, speaker agents, even administrative assistants and summer interns. Mapping out those positions at any one company, especially a large corporation, could take you months.

So how do you know whom to reach out to? Every company is different. If a company has a speaker series, you should be able to send a few emails and figure out who runs the series, and make sure they check out your website. If a company is having an off-site, executive retreat, or internal or external event, it becomes much harder. Figuring out who books speakers is the most challenging part of corporate speaking, and it is why speaker agencies have long dominated the industry. Their contacts are invaluable, and some companies lazily just reach out to an agent when they're looking for a speaker. When you don't have an agent and you're breaking into the industry, your best bet is to do your research, mine your LinkedIn contacts, and ask around until you find the person at an organization who has the power to invite you to speak.

For most tech and business conferences, it's much easier. Go to the conference's website, click on the Speakers tab, and you'll find a Call for Speakers page or an application form or contact information. If you're too late to apply for this year's event, just email the conference organizer and start a conversation about speaking at next year's event.

One quick note: the path to your gatekeeper might surprise you. I've taught two workshops at Esalen Institute, one of the most prestigious (and beautiful) personal growth retreat centers in the world, located on the Pacific Ocean, in Big Sur, California. How did I get to teach at Esalen? Because my sister's friend was a massage therapist at Esalen. My sister gave her friend a copy of my self-published book, which she really enjoyed, and (without me even asking) my sister's friend shared it with Esalen's program director. You never know who will unlock the key to your gate.

## Exercise: Lead generation

This exercise will help you build your speaking leads. To begin, open a new Speaking Leads spreadsheet in Excel or Google Sheets.

1. Make a list of 10 conferences you want to speak at this year. On your spreadsheet, note the dates of the conference, the conference organizer's name and email if you have it, where the conference is located, and a speaker application deadline if they have one. When you have time, submit an application to speak at these 10 conferences.

2. Make a list of 10 friends you know well who work at companies or organizations you think would be interested in your talk. On your spreadsheet, note your friend's name, email, position, and the company they work for. When you have time, email your friends and see if they can put you in touch with someone at their company that plans events or books speakers for lunch talks, workshops, executive retreats, or company conferences. If they can't, or don't know this person, ask if they know someone else who might!

3. Make a list of 10 speaker-friends you know well who have spoken at conferences or companies you're interested in speaking at. On your spreadsheet, note your friend's name, email, and where they spoke. You can usually find out where people have spoken from their website, or by following them on social media. When you have time, email your friends and ask them if they would be willing to make a connection to the conference organizer or company they spoke at. Note: this is a huge ask, especially if you are a new, relatively inexperienced speaker asking a more experienced speaker to introduce you to a corporate client of theirs. Do not be surprised if some speakers say they can't make an intro for you. Thank them anyway. They may prefer to make the intro after you've built up more experience and credibility. Even if some speakers turn you down, you should be able to make a few connections this way.

And just like that, you have dozens of new speaking leads. I recommend doing this exercise every few months to make sure you're developing your lead pipeline.

# 38

# Stay in touch with your leads

**AS PEOPLE START TO REACH OUT** to you about speaking, and as you start to reach out to conferences and companies, it's important to keep a list of your industry contacts. I have a Google Doc that I add to every time I receive or write an email about speaking. It includes the contact's name, email, company, position, where the gig is located, and the date of when we last communicated. If I end up speaking somewhere, I color the row green, and if the gig doesn't come through, I make the row red. If I haven't heard back from the organizer, I color the row yellow. Every few months I go through my list of leads and see if there are any yellow contacts I haven't spoken to in a long time, and I shoot them an email that says:

"Hey [INSERT NAME], I hope things are going well at [INSERT COMPANY]. It's been a few months since we talked about me speaking at [INSERT EVENT]. I wanted to check in and see if you had any upcoming events or opportunities that I might be a good fit for. Here are a few things I've been up to recently [link to a new video of a talk, or an article I've published].

I look forward to talking to you about collaborating soon.

I've gotten gigs simply from checking in with a client I haven't spoken to in months. Sometimes they say, "I'm so glad you reached out! We have an upcoming event that you'd be a perfect fit for." Of course, sometimes they don't respond or they say, "Hey, unfortunately there's nothing on the radar right now." As long as you're respectful and don't bombard someone's inbox (I recommend checking in with your leads every four or five months or so), staying in touch with your leads is a good way to cultivate new opportunities.

# 39

# Not all gigs are created equal

**THERE ARE MANY DIFFERENT** types of speaking engagements. When you're building your speaking business, you will likely end up with each of these types of gigs, plus others. Here's a breakdown of what to expect, with an important caveat that every gig is different, every speaker is different, speaking fees vary widely, and you may end up making much less money than this—or much more.

**Meet-ups and in-kind gigs: Meet-up groups, co-working spaces, happy hour gatherings, places like General Assembly and WeWork, tiny (broke) nonprofits, your friends' organizations**
Your goals: Get practice, gain credibility, spread your message, build your email list, get referrals for future gigs, get media assets
Financial target: Anything greater than $0 is a bonus

**Gigs you create yourself: Host a workshop or a retreat, host your own free event**

Your goals: Get practice, sell from the stage authentically and effectively, get people to buy your products (coaching, consulting, books, courses, etc.), build your email list, get referrals for future gigs, get media assets

Financial target: Depends on your business

**Educational gigs: Colleges, universities, small-to-medium sized cause-based organizations and nonprofits**

Your goals: Inspire the audience, gain credibility, get a testimonial, get referrals for future gigs, get media assets

Financial target: $3,000-$5,000

**Conference gigs: Panels, TEDx events, SXSW, small tech and business conferences (ticket price under $1,000)**

Your goals: Network with other attendees, establish your expertise by being on a panel, get corporate leads and referrals from conference organizers and audience members, get a testimonial, get high-quality video and other media assets

Financial target: $0-$3,000 plus expenses (flight, hotel, transportation, meals) but expect to only get your expenses covered

**Corporate gigs: Large companies, associations, large (well-resourced) nonprofits, high-profile corporate events, large tech and business conferences (ticket price**

**over $1,000), executive leadership retreats, summits, all-hands company meetings, workshops, trainings**

Your goals: Get paid, demonstrate your worth, make your client happy, establish expertise, get high-quality video and other media assets, get a testimonial, get referrals

Financial target: Less experienced corporate speakers: $3,000-$5,000 plus expenses; more experienced corporate speakers $5,000-$20,000+ plus expenses; rate depends on your experience.

# 40

# The money is in the uncool

**THE COOLEST COMPANIES** and conferences often don't pay speakers. If you want to make money, find the lamest possible companies and the conferences your friends have never heard of.

Instagram and the digital nomad scene have misguided many speakers. They incorrectly assume that every gig is going to be on the beach somewhere at a fancy resort. If you're lucky, you will occasionally get invited to speak at conferences in tropical locations—this past fall I got invited to speak at a resort in Aruba and it was awesome! But most gigs are going to be in old Marriot hotel conference rooms, in cities you've never heard of, for colleges and companies and associations you didn't even know existed. This is the life of a speaker who actually makes a living from public speaking.

Let me give you a personal example. For the past four years, I've tried unsuccessfully to get gigs at Airbnb, Twitter, and Square. I've lived in San Francisco for six years and know numerous people who work at these companies, so it's frustrating that I haven't been able to break in. However, even when I talked to someone about speaking at Square, they said they wouldn't be able to pay me (which is ironic since Square is worth about $17 billion).

I'm not sure exactly why it is that the coolest, wealthiest, most innovative companies don't like to pay speakers, but one hypothesis I have is that they don't feel like they need to. Any speaker would kill to put the Airbnb logo on their website, so they have leverage. Or perhaps, specifically for my topic, these companies are all set. They literally employ thousands of millennials, and they probably already have a dozen millennial workplace experts on staff, so their need for my services is low.

Contrast this with a well-paid gig I did with The Symposium of Community Bank Directors in Phoenix, Arizona. I bet you've never heard of them. It's a gathering of small community banks from the western region of the country. The Symposium of Community Bank Directors couldn't be more different than Square. They're like the Square of one hundred years ago. But you know what? Community banks are still really popular and do a lot of important work, and they are trying to better reach a millennial audience, so they were in need of my services.

The point is: the places where you want to speak are not often the places that want you. For my business, I've learned to avoid the hottest tech companies in favor of companies and organizations that are struggling with recruiting and retaining millennial talent. That's not going to be Airbnb and their cool office and endless stream of free kombucha on tap. It's going to large, old-school, less popular companies, struggling to attract the next generation of workers.

If you give talks on wellness and mindfulness, my advice would be to avoid the coolest, most "mindful" organizations, and target the ones where employees are suffering the most from burnout and stress. Don't try to speak at Google or on Oprah's SuperSoul Sunday or at a Deepak Chopra event. Instead, try speaking to the U.S. Army or a Wall Street hedge fund. If you give talks on creativity and innovation, look beyond the hottest creativity conferences like Summit Series, Collision, and World Domination Summit, and find the most boring, least innovative events in the least interesting locations. Speak at an insurance brokers association or an annual tax accounting convention—because that's where they need your message most. And that's probably the place that actually has the budget to pay you real money. You may think I'm joking, but do a quick Google search for upcoming accounting-related conferences this year. There are literally *hundreds*, and each of them needs someone like you to make their event more interesting.

Wannabee Speakers are excited about speaking at their friend's event in Tulum, México (that's gonna *cost them* money to attend). Breakthrough Speakers are happy to travel to suburban Phoenix to be paid thousands of dollars an hour for a gig. Breakthrough Speakers know that the money is in the uncool.

# 41

# This is an association nation

**ONE OF THE BEST MARKETS** for paid public speaking is trade associations. Last fall I spoke at a wonderful event called ASAE: Associations@Work in Baltimore, about creating a purpose-driven workplace. ASAE is a network of professional association members. Yes, it's an *association of associations*! Which basically means that every single person in the audience is someone that could potentially book me to come speak at their association. It's like the Super Bowl of corporate speaking. Did you know there are hundreds of professional associations in America? Each one of those associations has (at least one) annual conference which is made up of members who work at organizations that often book speakers as well.

Here are just a few examples to help you see how vast this industry is: there is an Association of Postconsumer Plastic Recyclers, the Global Business Travel Association, the National Association of Printing Ink Manufacturers, the National Academy of Elder Law Attorneys, the

National Organization for the Reform of Marijuana Laws, the Flexible Packaging Association, the National Coalition of Black Meeting Planners, the Association of Catholic Publishers, the International Association of Hospitality Accountants, the Metal Building Manufacturers Association, the Jewish War Veterans of the United States, and the Western Golf Association. There are hundreds of associations out there. Now, your material is not going to be relevant to all of them. But the associations industry is a great place for you to find gigs.

A quick note on associations: most of them are nonprofits. But this doesn't mean you shouldn't charge your full speaking rate. In fact, many associations have large event budgets and big budgets to pay speakers. As Antonio Neves once posted in the Facebook group for The Women Speaker Initiative,

**"I see a lot of people getting hung up on the 'nonprofit' subject on some threads regarding payment, as if they should immediately discount your speaking fee. Not so. Let's be clear, many nonprofits are extremely well run; support amazing causes; pay their people well; have nice budgets, etc. Public financial records are available for nonprofits on their site and you can learn a lot from them. Some of my largest paydays have been from nonprofits (i.e., trade associations) and this has not hurt them, their mission or cause. In fact, your message may help them go farther and reach more people."**

# 42

# A rant on conferences that don't pay speakers fairly

**WHEN I FIRST STARTED SPEAKING,** I probably did close to 50 speaking engagements before receiving a check for one of my gigs. Some people advise artists and creatives to never work for free, but I think the truth is that in the speaking industry, it's impossible to build up your experience, contacts, and industry credibility without speaking for free, especially when you're first getting started.

However, I also know there are conferences and companies that take advantage of speakers—especially women and people of color speakers. Even when women and people of color are actually booked to speak, they are consistently underpaid when compared to their colleagues.

In one experience, I was a co-emcee for an event where a woman of color speaker was unpaid, while a white dude (me) who did the exact same amount of work, and had the same qualifications as her, was paid several thousand dollars. This wasn't an evil corporation either—it was a purpose-driven leadership conference that prides itself on valuing diversity and social impact. When I asked my female colleague if she had received her $3,000 check for being a co-emcee, she said, "What check? They didn't tell me it was paid, and I didn't even think to ask to get paid."

In that instance, I said something to the CEO and the organization ended up paying the female speaker what they paid me. Usually, when I ask my women speaker friends what they were paid for a speaking gig, it is significantly less than what I was paid for similar engagements. This is messed up and it needs to stop—and it's the reason I launched The Women Speaker Initiative. Obviously, a speaker with ten years of experience (or a speaker who is famous or a bestselling author), is going to be paid more than someone who has zero experience, but that doesn't justify some of the inconsistencies I've experienced when it comes to the gender and race pay gap in public speaking.

# 43

# A rant on conferences that only book white dudes to speak

**SO WHY ARE SO MANY** Boring Old White Dudes (BOWDs) getting booked to speak if they aren't great speakers? When people get power they usually give the power back to people they know—basically, BOWDs invite (and pay) other BOWDs to speak. In other words, it's patriarchy, sexism, and racism, plain and simple. Public speaking has always been a prestigious field and many conference organizers and corporate bookers are clearly biased, consciously or unconsciously, to assume that white men are more worthy of giving talks in front of large audiences than women or people of color.

Many conference organizers (both male and female) will often say it's hard to find women speakers because there aren't a lot of women in leadership positions. In my opinion, this is a tired excuse. If you can't find a talented woman to speak at your event, ask around. I guarantee you someone in your network can recommend scores of brilliant female CEOs and leaders who are incredible on stage. It's high time we stop overlooking all of the accomplished women and people of color who are CEOs, professors, business leaders, politicians, authors, and thought leaders.

One study found that men gave more than twice as many talks as women at the top universities in the United States (69 percent to 31 percent). Rice University's Michelle Hebl and Christine Nittrouer found that this wasn't because there are simply more men working in academia, but that the process by which speakers are selected is subject to discriminatory biases. Ed Young writes in *The Atlantic*, "The team estimated the full pool of available speakers by counting every professor in their six chosen fields at each of the top 100 U.S. universities [biology, bioengineering, political science, history, psychology, and sociology]. And even after adjusting for the relative numbers of men and women in the various fields or ranks, they found that men are *still* 20 percent more likely to be invited to give colloquium talks than women."

For those of you thinking, "Well, maybe it's because women don't want to give talks—maybe they'd prefer to stay at home with their families," the study also disproved that biased explanation, finding that women want to give talks just as much as men, see speaking as valuable for their careers, and are no more likely to decline talks because of family obligations.

So clearly, the problem isn't the fact that there aren't enough qualified women to speak. It's simply that women aren't being invited as frequently as men. And the problem is even worse for women of color speakers. A University of California Hastings study, based on interviews of 60 women of color in STEM fields and a survey of 557 women found that a full 100 percent of women of color reported gender bias. Black women in STEM were more likely (77 percent) than other women (66 percent) to report "having to prove themselves over and over again," so as hard as it is for women to break through to the main stage, it's even harder for women of color.

# 44

# 3 simple ways that all speakers can get more women and people of color on stage

1. **Nominate.** Michelle Kim, the co-founder and CEO of Awaken, which provides experiential diversity, inclusion, and equity workshops that empower managers and teams to lead inclusively, advises leaders to "use your power to level the playing field." When you get asked to speak at a conference or event, see who else is on the line-up. If you are available, accept the invitation and recommend at least 3 women/ people of color you know that are amazing speakers to the conference organizer. If you aren't available, you should still recommend 3 women/POC you know that are amazing speakers. They might not take everyone,

but they might select 1-2 folks, and consider others the following year.

2. **Speak up, then step back.** If you are a white dude and get invited to speak on a panel with only other white dudes, speak up. If you are a white dude and get invited to speak at an event with zero or too few women/POC speakers, speak up. Refuse to speak at the event, unless they invite more women/POC speakers. If you are a white woman and get invited to speak on a panel with only other white people, speak up. Refuse to do the panel, unless they invite more POC/folks representing marginalized groups onto the panel. If you don't know any women/POC who would be a fit for the event, ask other women/POC in your community. Also, pro tip: when you're actually on the panel, speak second (or fourth). Talk less, listen more, and let someone else have the first word!

3. **Do the work.** Maintain and subscribe to lists of speakers of diverse genders, races, sexual orientations, nationalities, backgrounds, and experiences. Remember that many conference organizers are busy and under pressure. Make it as easy as possible for them to find other speakers. Maintain a spreadsheet with recommended speakers, and include their name, email, website, topic of expertise, and city of residence. For some recommended lists, check out the Resources section (see: The Women's Speaker

Initiative, FRESH Speakers, More Women's Voices, Tech Inclusion, 1000 Tech and Science Speakers Who Aren't CIS Men).

# 45

# 3 simple ways that all conference organizers and event planners can get more women and people of color on stage

1. **Be honest and make the ask.** If your line-up is a little too male or a little too white, admit it. Don't try to act like people won't notice, they will. Be vulnerable and transparent. Ask for help. Post a call for speakers on LinkedIn, Facebook and Twitter. Make it known that you want to do better. Ask your friends and social media network to suggest amazing women and POC leaders, speakers, and storytellers. If your friends don't have recommendations, ask them to ask their friends. If those people can't help,

keep asking. Don't ever say, "We tried to find more women and POC speakers, but there weren't any." That excuse is bullshit.

2. **Expand your network and your community.** As the documentary *Miss Representation* shows, "you can't be what you can't see." You also aren't likely to hire or promote or nominate or book someone you don't know, either. If you don't have a lot of brilliant women and POC in your professional or personal network, it's time to expand your professional and personal network. Change the types of events you're going to, read more books and articles by authors that don't look you, and follow new people on social media. Jenny Sauer-Klein, a master facilitator and founder of The Culture Conference, recommends that event planners, "tap leaders from the communities you want to attract to be on your advisory board, or to be ambassadors for your event. Ask them for recommendations and referrals and to put the word out to their communities. Give them a leadership role in your curating team and organization."

3. **Use the resources available.** Subscribe to lists of speakers of diverse genders, races, sexual orientations, nationalities, backgrounds, and experiences. Don't just post a call for speakers on your own website or social media, put your call for speakers out to

groups filled with women and people of color. For some recommended lists, check out the Resources section (see: The Women Speaker Initiative, FRESH Speakers, More Women's Voices, Tech Inclusion, 1000 Tech and Science Speakers Who Aren't CIS Men).

# 46

# When should you speak for free?

1. **When you're just getting started in your speaking career**

   If you are just getting started in your speaking career, your primary goal should be experience not money. I want you to get paid, but I also don't think it's reasonable to expect to be paid a lot of money if you've never been paid to speak before. As a rule of thumb, you should probably expect to do at least 10-15 unpaid formal speaking engagements before asking for serious money. I did 50 unpaid gigs before receiving a check, which was probably too many, and I wish I had started asking for money sooner.

2. **When you're speaking at (most) conferences**

   Conferences almost never pay speakers, unless they are top business conferences sponsored by a major brand, association or financial institution. And some of those often only pay the top level of speaker. Most tech conferences, innovation conferences, social impact conferences, nonprofit conferences, and other startup-y conferences don't usually pay speakers (beyond travel and expenses).

The key is to make the determination on whether it's worth your time and energy based on the potential connects, exposure, expertise, travel, etc. Who will you meet there? What relationships will you build? Are you in front of a room of potential buyers for your offering? Is it your target demographic? Do you want to travel to the location where the conference is and make a vacation out of it?

I have spoken for free in front of a room of 100 HR officers (my exact target demographic) and booked more than five speaking gigs, totaling over $40,000 of dollars of revenue from the unpaid gig. So, yes, damn straight it was worth it. In fact, many of the gigs I've booked on referral have been from unpaid conferences or events. Conferences are an essential source of lead generation for speakers. If you want to be in the public speaking business, I advise you to speak at conferences for free, especially if you're going to be in front of people who could book you for a future gig. Now, I don't advise you not to ask for money. You should always ask for money. But many conferences (something like 90 percent of them) don't pay speakers.

If you turn down conferences since they aren't paying, it's going to be hard to build your speaking business. Many of these conferences are not in good shape financially. They're not the ones with the money. The real money in corporate speaking is in the companies. And the people from the companies go to the conferences. Get the money from the companies by going to the conferences.

Remember: just because a conference doesn't pay you to speak, doesn't mean they shouldn't cover your expenses for getting to the conference. If I do a conference that doesn't pay a fee, I still expect the conference to cover my basic expenses: travel, lodging, the conference registration, ground transportation, etc. If a conference isn't paying you to speak and isn't going to cover any of your expenses, you need to think about whether it's worth it for you considering that you're going to end up *losing money* on the gig.

3. **When you're speaking at a nonprofit that truly has no budget or a friend's organization or doing a personal favor for a colleague or organization you care about**

   Even though I charge around $10,000 for a corporate speaking gig and have been speaking for three years, I usually do not charge small or struggling nonprofits, or organizations run by close friends or colleagues, or organizations with a social mission I am deeply passionate about. There are some exceptions to this rule, but I know speakers who have been speaking for 10+ years who regularly speak for free if the cause is worthy. Every speaker has to make their own decision about when it's appropriate to charge and how much to charge, which is an even harder decision when you know an organization lacks financial resources.

# 47

# Money does not always come in the form of a check. Money is who's in the room.

**HERE ARE TWO EXAMPLES** that will help you think about whether to take an unpaid gig.

**Example 1.** The first example is when I spoke at Culture Summit in 2016. Culture Summit is one of the leading company culture gatherings in the country. It brings together people who work in the human resources space, people who are dedicated to hiring and retaining top talent, and who care about best practices for employee engagement. The conference was also organized by two friends I know from San Francisco, Hung Pham and Vanessa Shaw. When Hung and Vanessa asked if I would deliver my "Building a Purpose-Driven Workplace" key-note at Culture Summit, of course I was interested. When they said they didn't have a budget to cover a speaking fee, I was still happy to participate. Why? Because I knew there would be people in the room who cared about my topic and who worked at companies that could potentially book me to speak. Good thing I listened to my instinct. One of the audience members was an employee engage-ment specialist at MailChimp. She loved my talk and after a series of emails, she invited me to be a keynote speaker at MailChimp's Coffee Hour (previous speakers for this series include Big Boi, Brené Brown, Ann Friedman, and Congressman John Lewis—people *way* cooler than me). To date, the MailChimp engagement is the most presti-gious (and well-paid) opportunity I've ever had.

**Example 2.** The second example is when a successful venture-backed start-up reached out to me to speak, but told me they didn't have a speaker budget. I checked their Wikipedia page and read an article about them in Tech-Crunch and realized they had raised over $300 million in venture funding and had a fancy office in downtown San Francisco. I thought to myself, "If $300 million is enough to pay for catered lunch for your employees every day, it should probably be enough to pay me—or at least pay me something." Can you imagine if this start-up went to buy pizza for their employees and the pizza place said, "That'll be $500," and they responded, "Oh, we don't have a budget to cover food. We're a start-up." I think the pizza place would be like, "You can go fuck yourself."

Well, that's essentially what this company was saying to me: "We want your services for free."

I decided to turn down the unpaid gig, not because they didn't want to pay me (although that annoyed me), but more importantly because there were no potential new clients in the room. The audience was going to be employees of this start-up, and while it would have been great to deliver my message to these employees and help them find more purpose in their work, no one in the audience was in a position to bring me to their company to speak (because they already were employed by this start-up).

In short, make a decision about whether to take an unpaid gig based on who's in the room. The truth is, I'd almost pay to speak in front of a full room of potential buyers. In fact, the academic market works like this. Speakers often have to apply to speak at college conferences like the Association of Fraternal Leadership & Values (AFLV) and National Association for Campus Activities (NACA), and if their program is accepted, the speaker still has to pay both for conference registration and the travel costs for the conference. When I was trying to book gigs at colleges, I spoke at AFLV in Indianapolis, which cost me about $1,000 in airfare, hotel, meals, and conference fees. But, I ended up booking two gigs from my talk, which earned me more than $5,000. So, the investment was worth it.

# 48

# There is no such thing as an unpaid gig

**LET'S SAY A CONFERENCE** or client simply doesn't have a budget to pay you a speaking fee. Especially when you're starting out, you're going to do plenty of unpaid gigs. Hopefully, they still cover your travel and expenses. But what else can you ask for to make an unpaid gig worth your time? I recommend you try to get some or all of the following assets for every gig you do, especially gigs that are not financially lucrative:

- A high-quality video of your talk
- A testimonial from the client for your website
- High-quality photos from your talk
- Referral from the organizer to 2-3 colleagues who might be interested in your talk
- A blog post on the conference/organization's website about you
- Social media posts by the conference/organization about you

- Start a conversation with the client about returning to give a paid talk/workshop in the future

As lawyer and impact strategist Avery Blank, who speaks frequently to organizations about leadership, women, millennials, and strategic positioning, likes to say, "You have value. You are giving your time and sharing your knowledge. Don't discredit or undermine what you have to offer. If you don't see and advocate for your value, no one else will. Don't be a doormat. Know your worth, and ask for it."

Another friend of mine, Amy Lazarus, the founder and CEO of InclusionVentures, has been speaking for ten years on topics related to inclusion, diversity, leadership, unconscious bias, and dialogue. She mentioned that her organization has different pricing depending on the size and sector of the client. "When I was first starting InclusionVentures, I got some of the best advice from Nicolette Pizzitola of Compasspoint Partners," Amy recalls.

**"[Nicolette] said if I wanted to provide a workshop or speaking for a reduced price or for free, to say: 'Typically my fees are $X. I love the work of your organization and I'd like to be able to support you. I'm willing to do this for a reduced fee and in exchange, I ask that I can use your logo, that you provide a testimonial I can use on my website, and that you introduce me**

to three people/organizations that may have budget for this.'"

Amy has applied this strategy for her own work, and has shared Nicolette's advice with countless entrepreneurs. She explains that clients or potential clients are willing to do these small lifts that go a long way.

# 49

# When it comes to asking for money, remember these rules

1. **Most importantly (for speaking—and for life!): you matter and your story matters.** Don't ever forget this and don't ever let anyone ever tell you differently. Asking for money indicates that you value yourself and the value you bring to an audience.

2. **Speaking is not like other jobs.** You are not quoting a fee for the 15-minute or 30-minute or 60-minute talk you are giving, you're quoting a fee for the hours, months, and years of research, writing, and professional experience that give you the ability to get on stage and say something meaningful. As my friend Vanessa Shaw, founder of Human Side of Tech, reminds people: charge a day rate. She says, "Think about your work as the value you bring, not the hours. People charge $30,000/hour because of the value their presence and

experience brings. Not because of how much time they give. Never ever charge by the hour."

When I tell friends I get paid $10,000 for a corporate keynote that's usually 45-minutes, they are like, "Holy shit, you make $10K an hour, that's incredible!" On the one hand, this is true. I do get paid $10K an hour, which is dope. On the other, I'm able to charge that because I've spent more than four years writing two books (that's over 100,000 words), interviewing hundreds of millennials, writing over 100 published articles and blog posts, and delivering more than 200 formal talks about millennials in the workplace, speaking to a total audience of more than 50,000 people. I also don't get paid $10K every time I speak. So, when you think about it like that, $10K for an hour seems a lot more reasonable, and Simon Sinek or Brené Brown charging five times that (or more) for a keynote is justified based on their experience, exposure and prior success (they've sold millions of books, their talks have millions of views, and their insights have had a profound impact on millions of people and organizations).

3. **No two gigs are created equal, no two speakers are created equal, and no two speakers are coming to a gig from the same place.** There is not one answer for how much you should charge for a gig. If you ask for money, a client may give you what you ask for, they may

give you less, and they may say they have no money to pay you. Every single speaker has to decide for themselves when to take an unpaid gig, and whether it's worth it based on the relationship building, exposure, and potential networking opportunities.

When I started speaking, I did around 50 unpaid engagements before I ever received a check for speaking. I'm not saying everyone should do that—I wish I had been paid for some of those, but doing those unpaid gigs gave me the experience, confidence, videos, marketing assets, connections, and referrals to get paid gigs and build my career. Every speaker is at a different spot in their career and it's important to remember that one person's unpaid gig at their friend's co-working space is another person's main stage TED talk. One person's first ever $500 gig, is another person's first ever $20,000 gig.

Of course, this *does not* justify unequal pay based on gender, race, or other factors, but you should expect to see different speakers getting paid very different amounts based on their experience, platform level, and the nature of the gig.

4. **The best way to get paid more money is to speak more often.** The more you speak, and the busier your calendar is, the more your speaking fee will grow. As Charlotte Raybourn, who runs Charlotte Raybourn Speaker Management and is the president of the

International Association of Speakers Bureaus, told me at 3 Ring Circus, "The best form of marketing is your speech itself."

# 50

# What you should charge for speaking fees?

**BEFORE YOU NEGOTIATE** a speaking fee with a client, think about these questions: *Have you been paid to speak before? How many times have you been paid to speak? What is the most you've ever been paid to speak? What's your average speaking fee? Who is the client? Is it a large corporation, a tiny conference, or a college or nonprofit or friend's organization? How many people will be in the audience?*

As I mentioned earlier, there is no right answer for what you should charge for a gig. Every speaker (and every gig) is different. To give you some fee ranges, my standard corporate speaking fee (often called an honorarium) is $10,000 for a 30-60 minute keynote (plus all expenses). Expenses for a domestic out-of-town gig usually run me about $1,000-$1,500 (round-trip airfare, hotel for 1-2 nights, meals, transportation, and miscellaneous travel expenses). In order to feel comfortable charging $10,000 plus a $1,000 travel fee, I've been speaking full-time for more than two years, have given more than 200 formal talks in front of large audiences, and spent over a year mostly speaking for free to practice (around 50 engagements) before I started charging money.

The most I've ever been paid to speak is $20,000 for a 45-minute keynote. I know some corporate speakers who make $25,000-$35,000 a gig, and I know some who make about $5,000. I often do talks that pay in the $6,000-$8,000 range. My small nonprofit and college/educational fee is in the $3,000-$5,000 range. If it's for an organization that truly has no money or a friend's organization or an organization whose mission I support deeply, I usually do those gigs for free.

When I first started charging for speaking, my fee was around $2,000-$3,000. While you should figure out a rate that feels good to you, I think that $3,000 is a good place to start once you've had at least 10-15 formal unpaid speaking engagements to practice. After you've done more engagements, you can bump up your rate to $3,000-$5,000, and then to $6,000-$8,000, and then $10,000, and higher. After you reach over $10,000, how fast (or slow) you should increase your rate really depends on your experience/platform, and how your keynote compares to similar speakers in your market.

In an article for *Harvard Business Review*, Dorie Clark, marketing strategist, professional speaker, and author of *Entrepreneurial You*, breaks down the following speaking fee ranges as a general rule of thumb:

- $500–$2,500 (for new speakers)
- $5,000–$10,000 (for beginning speakers, or those just establishing a brand with their first book)
- $10,000–$20,000 (for speakers with several books and other big career accomplishments)
- $20,000–$35,000 (for bestselling authors and professionals who are very well-known in their field)

Here are speaking fees (at least, according to information that's publicly available online, which may vary or not be up-to-date) of several speakers you may have heard of:

- Twyla Tharp: $30,000-$50,000
- Brené Brown: $50,000+
- Gary Vaynerchuk: $75,000+
- Barack Obama: $400,000

Please note there is no one-size-fits-all model or universal rule for speaker pricing and that some large companies—even reputable organizations—don't pay speaking fees, or they pay well below standard corporate rates. In fact, recently I agreed to do a talk for a corporate client that didn't have a budget, because I was going to be sharing the stage with one of my favorite authors, so I figured it was going to be worth it for me on a personal level.

Here are a few thoughts from my friend Kat Alexander

about how she approaches her speaking fees. Kat is the founder of Report It, Girl, and she speaks about overcoming trauma and healing from sexual violence.

**"When I'm asked to speak, I set up time for a call to hear more about what they're looking for, and then I say, "What's your budget?" In my experience, it only affirms that I am a professional. [In this case] UC Santa Barbara had money set aside, and I negotiated by saying, "I usually charge $3,500", which they accepted on the spot. I also spoke at a Domestic Violence event for $400, because that was their budget, and it was one of my first paid gigs—and yes, I want to support great nonprofit work. For me, it's a matter of standing in my worth and value, knowing that the content I've created and deliver has taken years to research. I'm mindful of how women are so often underpaid, especially for emotional labor—which my talks require because I speak about healing from trauma."**

I love how Kat stresses the importance of "standing in your worth and value." This is essential (and incredibly challenging), especially for people who have not been told how great they are their entire lives. As a straight cisgender white dude, no one has ever told me I can't do something. The media has supported this notion, with infinite examples of white guys like me doing pretty much anything they want (and getting pretty much anything they want), on stage, on screen, in magazines, in books, online, anywhere and everywhere. The same cannot be said for women, people of color, the LGBTQ community, and other marginalized people.

Stepping into your power happens when you write your story. It happens on stage when you share your story, but it also happens when you get on the phone with a client and confidently say, "My name is _____. My rate is _____. I am worth it." As Amy Lazarus of Inclusion-Ventures likes to say, "There is money out there, and it is going to other people. Ask for it."

## Exercise: Stand in your worth

I know it's not easy to ask for money. I know this because I've been making a living from public speaking the past three years, and I still have trouble asking for money. But, I've gotten better at it. If you're having trouble getting psyched up to make the ask to get paid for a speaking gig, here's a little exercise.

Stand in front of a mirror and say this 10 times:
My name is _____. I am worth it.
My speaking rate is _____. I am worth it.

Still not fired up?

Go into your closet and put on your favorite outfit. The outfit you feel most yourself in. Then, blast your favorite song as loud as you can. If you can't think of a song, try something by Beyoncé or Robyn. Now stand in front of your mirror and say this 10 times:

My name is \_\_\_\_\_. I am worth it.

My speaking rate is \_\_\_\_\_. I am worth it.

Now you're definitely ready to ask for more money.

# 51

# Speaking rates for panels, fireside chats, workshops, and webinars

**YOUR GOAL AS A CORPORATE SPEAKER** should be to book as many keynotes as possible. Keynotes command the highest speaking rates. Panels, as you know from speaking at conferences, rarely pay anything beyond expenses. Fireside chats are becoming much more popular for conferences and events, because the audience enjoys seeing the speaker deliver un-rehearsed remarks and being asked questions they've never been asked before. If you get invited to do a fireside chat, your rate should be similar to what you would charge for a keynote.

What about workshops? Workshops usually require the speaker to prepare far more material in advance than a keynote or fireside chat. Workshops are also usually longer than a keynote, and can sometimes be 90 minutes, or even a half-day or full-day. For these workshops, make sure you factor in the amount of prep time required for your fee. Generally, when speakers and facilitators tell me what they charge for a workshop, I tell them they should double their rate. Too often, speakers undercharge for workshops. For a workshop, I recommend charging at least 100-125 percent of your keynote honorarium.

Webinars, in my opinion, are the least optimal type of speaking engagement. Some companies like them because they think they can get a speaker to deliver content without paying their full fee, or without having to cover their travel to the office. But webinars are rarely an effective way to connect with an audience. Have you ever heard someone say, "That webinar changed my life! It was the most amazing 60 minutes of my life! Best talk I've ever seen by far!"? No, you've never heard someone say that. This is because most webinars suck.

There is a high risk of having tech issues with the webinar software, and as a speaker, it's really difficult to deliver a great talk when you can't even see your audience. Some speakers don't ever do webinars for this reason. If you do, I recommend charging 50-75 percent of your keynote fee. Webinars make the most sense if you are unable to travel to a specific location, but still want to build a future relationship with a client. They also work very well for hosting your own lead generation events for finding clients to sell online products to. If you are the type of speaker that is selling your own coaching program, online course, or other product, you'll likely want to start hosting webinars to build your email list and lead pipeline.

# 52

# Always negotiate your speaking fee

**MOST OF THE REQUESTS I GET** to speak are inbound (the client is reaching out to me), and usually the client fills out the contact form on my website. I have a blank field on the contact form for "estimated speaker budget," but the client will often leave this field blank. As with any matters of salary negotiation, most clients don't want to name a fee and then realize they could have gotten away with paying you less (and you don't want to name a price and then realize the company was going to pay you twice what you quoted!), so here's the step-by-step plan I follow when negotiating a speaking fee for a paid engagement.

1. A client completes the contact form on my website (or emails me), indicating their interest in inviting me to speak. They let me know the date, the type of engagement, and who will be in the audience.

2. I do a little background research on the nature of the

speaking engagement. Is it a corporate client, a conference, a big start-up, a tiny start-up, a nonprofit that feeds the homeless? How many people will I be speaking to? Is this a high-profile event or a small event? How far do I have to travel for the event?

3. If I'm available for the date of the event, I respond to their email, letting them know I'm interested and would love to set up a time to discuss the details and budget on the phone. This is very important. Never discuss speaking fees over email. You're more likely to negotiate a higher rate on the phone.

4. Once on the phone, I ask for more details about the event and I talk to the client about my experience and why I'm an ideal fit for the gig. Remember: this call is still part of the sales process. You haven't signed a contract yet, so the client still isn't quite sure they want to book you. I've found that this sales call is essential to booking a gig: you have to make the client certain you're the right person for the gig. (Quick note: If I don't think I'm the right person for the gig because the client is looking for something that's not my area of expertise, I'm honest about this, and I recommend a speaker I know who is. Some speakers don't do this, but then they deliver an awful presentation and the client may speak poorly of them to their colleagues and other conference

organizers. It's best to be honest with yourself and your client.)

5. Assuming I'm a good fit, I ask the client what their budget range is. Sometimes they'll be direct and say, "Well, we're thinking $6K-$7K." In which case I respond with, "My standard corporate speaking fee is $10K plus a $1K travel fee." Then they might come back with $7,500, and we settle on $9K plus $1K expenses.

6. The client might ask you to quote your fee first. In this case, if it's a corporate client, I would say, "My standard corporate speaking fee is $10K, plus a $1K travel fee." In some instances, the client comes back and says, "That's within our range and works for us." In which case, great, I'm getting paid my full rate.

7. However, if I name my fee and the client says, "That rate is way too high for us. We're on a tight budget and can't go higher than $6K," first I double check if there is any wiggle room to negotiate. Can they do $8K? If they say, "Nope, we absolutely can't go higher than $6K, that's our total budget and we're already pushing it," I make a decision based on the factors we've already discussed.

   • First off, do I want the gig?

- Is this an opportunity that will be good for my career?
- Will speaking at this company help me book gigs at other companies?
- Most importantly: who will be in the room?

In most instances, I still take the $6K because that's still a sweet amount of money for 30-minutes of work, and because I'm still early in my speaking career. I can imagine once I've been speaking for 5+ years that I won't want to do gigs that don't pay me my full rate, but for now, I'm still primarily interested in gaining experience.

8. Once you've agreed on a fee, it's usually the speaker's job to draft a contract and make sure you include any relevant details on speaker fee, travel fees or reimbursements, the details of the engagement, and any additional appearances (videos, media interviews, podcasts, etc.) you'll be doing as part of the gig.

# 53

# Don't get greedy

**A QUICK WORD OF CAUTION:** don't get greedy with your speaking fees, especially as your fee starts to increase. I've done a few gigs for $6,000 or $7,000 when I probably could have charged $10,000, and charged $10,000 when I probably could have charged $15,000. Remember to play the long game. The more you have a reputation as a speaker that does a great job, for a reasonable fee given your experience level, the more likely you will get recommended for future gigs and build a speaking career that is long-lasting and sustainable.

In other words, would you rather do one gig for $15,000, but then never get booked again because the client didn't think you were actually worth $15,000, or do three gigs for $6,000, and have each one of those clients recommend you for two or three other gigs? I've booked a lot of gigs because a speaker's ego was too big to take a $6,000 gig, whereas I will happily get paid that amount of money for an hour's work.

There are a lot of speakers out there whose fees

are way too high given the mediocre quality of their presentation. It's far better to under-charge, over-perform, and make your client and future clients happy.

# 54

# You don't need a speaking agent—yet

**WHEN YOU'RE GETTING STARTED** with speaking and booking your first ten or fifteen paid speaking gigs, you're better off not using an agent. If you're just getting started, most speaking agents won't work with new speakers anyway, and most agents won't work with speakers making less than $5,000 (or for many, less than $10,000) per keynote. Just to put it in perspective, in the past two years, I've made about four times as much money from booking speaking engagements on my own, than from working with agents.

What does a speaking agent do? A speaker agent will usually come to a speaker saying they have a client who is interested in booking the speaker for a gig. In exchange for booking the gig, the speaker usually gives the agent 25 percent of their fee. The agent usually handles the contract and invoicing process, ensuring the client pays the speaker fee and reimburses for any expenses. A lot of speakers think having an agent means success, but if you're number 99 on an agency roster of 100 speakers in terms of importance to the agency, it doesn't mean much except for a cool Facebook post ("I'm so cool, I have a speaker agent!").

If you don't actually get booked for gigs, who cares if you have a speaking agent? If you're only getting one or two emails every couple months about speaking, you aren't ready for an agent.

Until speaking agencies are reaching out to you to book gigs and you're getting multiple speaking inquiries per month, my advice is to do it yourself. The exception to this would be niche industries and niche agencies. For example, Shift is an agency for educational programs/interactive workshops for high school and college audiences. I used to be with CAMPUSPEAK, a top college speaking agency. The college market is tricky and hard to break into, so if that's your focus, it makes sense to find a college speaking agent. I think agencies make sense for niche audiences if an agent is committed to selling you and already has established contacts that it would be very difficult or time consuming for you to find yourself.

When you do work with corporate speaking agents, I recommend doing so on a non-exclusive basis. An agent will ask me, "Can we book you for this great gig, we'll pay your full rate, and take a 25 percent cut?" I say, of course, since they are bringing me a gig I would never have gotten myself. But I would never sign an exclusive with an agency. An exclusive means every single gig you do (even if your best friend wants you to speak somewhere) would have to go through an agent and they would take a cut of your fee. Unless you're hella famous (like Oprah-level famous) or an agency is bringing you dozens of gigs a year, I don't think you should ever sign an exclusive with an agency.

If you've been speaking for several years, and are starting to command keynote fees of $10,000 or more, you might be ready to get considered for a top agency. Take a look at The Lavin Speaking Agency or the Washington Speakers Bureau. You'll start to notice some pretty famous people on there, so you might be like, "Damn, I know I'm a badass, but I'm not as cool as Reza Aslan or Margaret Atwood or Mark Manson!" The truth is you're not, and I'm not either, and that's okay! Have no fear, just keep practicing and you'll get to where you need to be. If you really want to humble yourself, take a look at The Harry Walker Agency website. They've got Hillary Clinton, Bill Clinton, and Shaquille O'Neal on there!

Patience, my friend. All in due time. Build it up. Gig by gig, as *Bird by Bird* author Anne Lamott might say. After booking gigs myself for over two years, I'm starting to do more work this year with SpeakInc, a leading speaking agency that has been in the business for 25 years, that I've really enjoyed working with. I like working with SpeakInc because they bring me well-paid opportunities that I would never be able to find on my own.

Remember: the speaking industry is old school. The advantage of working with a speaking agency is that they often have cultivated close personal relationships with event planners over many years, and these conference organizers and meeting planners trust the agents they've worked with before to provide talented speakers. Most event planners do not post open calls for their big keynote slots, because most event planners are too busy. They aren't willing to take a chance on a speaker that is an unknown quantity; they go directly to a speaker bureau they trust.

A few things to remember about working with speaker bureaus:

1. **Build personal relationships.** The more an agent knows your work and likes you as a whole person, the more likely they are to recommend you to their clients. The happier you make their clients, the happier agents are going to be to work with you.

2. **Be honest and respect the commission structure.** The speaker bureau business model is based on receiving 25 percent commission of your speaking fee. If an agent brings you a gig, and you book a new gig because of that original gig, you must *also* give the agent 25 percent of that spin-off gig as well. If you don't tell bureaus about a gig that you booked because of a gig they brought you, they'll probably find out anyway, be very upset, and likely never work with you again.

3. **Be patient.** In the short-term, you might be annoyed to give up 25 percent of your fee to an agent, but in five years, if they are booking you for 15-20 gigs a year, you are happily going to give them a cut of all that money they're bringing you. Nearly all of the top-grossing and top-performing professional speakers work with bureaus. Be smart and cultivate long-term mutually beneficial relationships with speaking bureaus and their partners.

I've listed several speaking bureaus in the Resources section that usually work with up-and-coming speakers on a non-exclusive basis. You might want to check out the marketing website eSpeakers, a site I use which allows you to post your booking information to several online speaker directories for a monthly fee. FRESH Speakers is a great forward-thinking agency for emerging new voices—they're one of the only agencies I've seen that doesn't have mostly old white dudes on their roster, and they are deeply committed to representing women, people of color, LGBTQ speakers, and other marginalized voices and stories.

# 55

# Don't get screwed: write your own contracts

**SOME COMPANIES OR EVENTS** will have a standard contract they use for booking speakers, but in many cases, you'll have to draft your own contract. While there is no single way to put together a speaking contract, here are six sections your contract should include. Once you've drafted a contract, send it to your contact to see if they have any questions or want to make any changes before signing.

1. Contract details
a) Define the two legal entities making this contractual agreement (the Organization's information and the Speaker's information).
b) Detail the specifics of the agreement being made between the two parties.

2. Cancellation details

a) Include a cancellation clause specifying that both parties are relieved of their obligations in case of a situation beyond their control (for example: inclement weather, sickness, physical disability, labor difficulties, war, epidemic, travel delays (including airline cancellations or delays), etc.

b) Include a clause that in the event of voluntary cancellation by the Organization for a reason not listed above, the Speaker will still be paid a percentage (usually 50 percent or more) of the agreed upon speaking fee. Some speakers will specify a specific date after which they are owed their entire fee, if an event is cancelled by the Organization.

3. Compensation details

a) Specify the speaking fee.

b) Specify any additional fee for travel and expenses or whether the Organization will be reimbursing the speaker's receipts for travel, hotel, meals, and other expenses.

c) Payment instructions and whether a late fee will be assessed after a certain amount of time.

4. Terms of Agreement. Specify whether additional appearances, seminars, discussion groups, lunches, press interviews, podcasts, media and social media arrangements, etc. will be included in the engagement. Specify usage rights to any photographs, videos, or other media or

social media assets, from the presentation. Many speakers like to specify that their presentation (and all presentation materials) will remain their intellectual property. Many speakers also like to specify any A/V requirements for their presentation.

5. Relationship of the parties and authorization. Define whether speaker is an independent contractor or employee of the Organization (usually an independent contractor).

6. Signatures, date, and contact information for you and the legal representative/signatory for the Organization.

# 56

# If you sell from the stage, focus on your value proposition

**THE FOCUS OF THIS GUIDE** is to help you book more corporate speaking engagements. However, many speakers use their public speaking skills to earn income without ever getting booked by a client. In other words, they create their own events and sell their own products from the stage, like coaching programs, online courses, books, consulting, or workshops. I know coaches who host free events where they offer a compelling presentation, give away a few tools for free, and then encourage people to sign-up for a $10,000 six-month coaching program at the end of the event. If they get ten people to sign up, they just made $100,000 in 60 minutes— that's a pretty sweet payday.

But selling from the stage takes a lot of practice and mastery. Not only do you need to be an expert public speaker, but your offer needs to provide tremendous value to the audience. There is nothing worse than watching an amateur speaker, who lacks any credentials, try to sell a half-baked product. I asked my friend Nate Bagley, a dating and relationships expert, about how to sell from the stage without being sleazy or inauthentic. Here's what he said:

If I'm selling from the stage, I create a product I think the audience would benefit from. I make an offer that often includes bonuses (extra value if you sign up today, like a free e-book, a mini-course, or access to a private FB group) and limiters (this is only available for X number of people). (These bonuses and limiters will help to get people who are on the fence to dip their toe in the water.) Then I make the offer and I shut up.

The goal is to provide something so valuable it has people sprinting to the back of the room. Some people try to use these tactics to manipulate people to buy. And sometimes that might work. But really the intent of the tools I use is to identify the people in the audience who need more of what I have to offer, and continue the conversation with them to see how I can serve them best.

The main mistake people make when selling from the stage is they don't rehearse their pitch enough. When you don't practice, you get nervous, you stumble over your words, and look desperate. You don't want to look desperate. Desperate people are takers. When you're prepared, you look polished and confident. You have the presence of someone who is ready to add value. And when you add value, dollars follow.

Get really clear on what value you can add to someone's life, what it's worth, and then rehearse your pitch over and over until it feels as comfortable as talking to your best friend.

Focus on the value proposition you're offering. Why should someone sign-up for your coaching program or take your online course? Recall your Speaker Zone of Genius, your Anchor, your Hook, and your Pain Point. Why you? Why your product? Why now?

Advanced speakers will sometimes book corporate gigs with clients, and then try to up-sell the audience members at their presentation. This means they're getting paid for a gig, and at that gig, their making money from selling additional products like coaching, courses, or consulting. So, instead of making $10,000 a keynote, suddenly they are potentially making $50,000 or more per gig. Before you do this, make sure it's okay with your client. Some companies and events will specifically not want you to sell from the stage during their events, as it can come off as tacky and unprofessional. Personally, I don't sell from the stage since I think it looks bad. I'd rather be known as a speaker that delivers great content than that guy who is going around hawking his product, "For a limited time only, you can get this product with my pale white face on it for $97, already marked down from $197, and previously marked down from $997, and there's only a few more spaces left, just sign up today!" I hate that crap. But, to each their own.

If you're an author-speaker, a great way to up-sell your client in a way that is both professional and adds value is selling bulk copies of your book. Whenever I book a corporate speaking gig, I ask if the client is interested in buying 100 copies of my book for the audience, and let them know I'm happy to individually sign books after the gig. Audience members love leaving events with a signed copy of a book—especially a signed book from the person they just saw give an amazing presentation. Depending on the client, you can also see if they are interested in booking you for a workshop (or consulting services) in addition to your keynote. This means you can deliver more content at each of your gigs, and charge more money.

I once met a popular speaker named Dan Ram, who was emceeing a conference I spoke at in Germany. Dan is based in Dublin, Ireland, and has hosted some of the largest tech conferences in the world, including SXSW, DLD, How to Web, Web Summit, and Bits and Pretzels. Dan told me that every time he emcees an event, he also offers consulting services to the conference organizer that include event design, agenda flow and logistics, and even speaker coaching and prep. I thought this was a brilliant up-sell; because Dan has spoken at so many tech conferences, he can offer his expertise in how to run a great event.

No two speakers are the same. You'll have to discover what works best when it comes to earning additional revenue from your speaking engagements.

# 57

# How to run your speaking business like a professional

**ONE OF THE BEST THINGS** about being a professional speaker is that you get to travel around the country and the world, and someone else covers your travel. How cool is that? Sometimes, in addition to getting your travel covered, you also receive an honorarium/speaking fee. In other words, you get paid to travel the world. What a dream. As you travel for business, I recommend getting a separate business credit card so you can easily track your business expenses. Keep track of these business expenses (and save your receipts), since most expenses while on business travel are tax-deductible.

In most cases, clients and events should cover the travel costs and expenses for your speaking gig. Common expenses include: round-trip airfare, hotel, ground transportation (Uber/Lyft, taxi, train, etc.), meals, wifi, and any other miscellaneous expenses. One way to handle expenses is to keep track of your receipts, include them on your invoice, and have your client reimburse you for expenses after the gig.

Another way is to add what's called a flat travel fee to your speaking fee. I recommend adding a $1,000-$1,500 flat travel fee to your speaking fee for a domestic speaking engagement (and $2,000-$2,500 for international gigs), instead of submitting expenses/receipts after a gig. So, for example if your speaking fee was $5,000, you'd charge the client a $5,000 speaking fee plus a $1,000 travel fee, or $6,000 total. No company wants to deal with processing all of your receipts for coffee, wi-fi on the airplane, Ubers, flights, and meals. Just add a flat travel/expenses fee to your speaking fee, and then make your own travel arrangements. Most events and clients should always book and cover your hotel room, since they are usually booking a block of hotel rooms anyway for a large event.

For my business, I set-up an LLC for my speaking business and elected to file taxes as an S-Corp, instead of signing contracts as a self-employed individual. Being an LLC protects me legally (in the unforeseen chance that me talking about millennials somehow leads to a lawsuit against me), and filing taxes as an S-Corp or C-Corp may offer tax deductions and savings that are not available to self-employed individuals. As with any matters financial or legal, I need to disclose that I am not qualified to give you formal financial or legal advice. Please consult a professional tax accountant, certified financial advisor, or attorney to see what makes sense for you and your business.

# 58

# Check in with the client a few weeks before the gig

**AFTER YOU'VE SIGNED A CONTRACT,** but a week or two before the gig itself, it's wise to have a check-in phone call with your client, just to make sure all the details are set. My old college speaking agency CAMPUSPEAK refers to this as the 'Happy Call' and it's a practice I've since incorporated into my speaking business. After all, the goal is to make sure your client is happy throughout the process of working with you. Here are a few details you'll want to clarify on your check-in call:

1. **Confirm the specifics.** Date, start time of your talk, length of your talk, time you'll be meeting the client, and the location of the gig. I can't tell you how many times I've booked a gig only to realize the day of the gig that I didn't know exactly where I was supposed to meet my contact. This is especially important on

college campuses. I once had a gig at Stanford University at the "student activities center," but realized when I got to Palo Alto that there are five different student activities centers at Stanford. Get the exact address where you're supposed to be.

2. **Know your audience.** Confirm who will be in the room, how many attendees are expected, the type of room you're speaking in, and how they plan on setting up the room. This is especially important if you're delivering an interactive workshop and you want the audience chairs to be set up in a circle instead of rows, or if you have any materials (whiteboards, Post-its, pens, paper) you want the client to provide. A great question to ask your client is: "Is there anything specific about your audience that I should know? Has anything significant happened at your office (or university) recently that folks have been talking about?"

3. **Do a tech check.** Make sure the client has your updated PowerPoint presentation. Confirm whether you're running off of their computer or your own laptop, that you have the correct adapters, slide clickers, and any specific requests for your microphone (wireless mic, or hand-held). When it's available, I always use a wireless lavalier microphone since that way I don't have to fumble around with the mic in one hand and the slide clicker in the other. Is there

anything else you want to be on stage, like a podium, chair, easel, or whiteboard?

4. **Get a cell phone number.** This is a small but important detail to remember. Often times you'll have had a phone call with a client on their office phone. Make sure you get a cell phone number for them, and at least one other colleague for any emergency phone calls you need to make. Let's say you're running late (never be late for a gig!) or your flight's delayed or there's a snowstorm or you're lost, you want to be able to call someone. Make sure the client has your cell number as well.

# 59

# Don't be a diva

**WHEN I ATTENDED NEW SPEAKER** training with CAMPUSPEAK, they stressed the importance of not being a diva. It was one of the best pieces of advice I ever received about public speaking. The public speaking business is filled with people who are more concerned with their Instagram presence and their elite airline status than actually delivering an insightful keynote. Don't be one of these douches. Just because someone pays you to speak somewhere does not mean you're a rockstar.

I once met this dude at a conference who spent the first two days of the conference bragging about how cool he was and how many Instagram followers he had and how he was about to close a book deal with a major publisher. Then he went on stage the next day and didn't even have a talk prepared. He was the worst speaker of the whole weekend and honestly, I bet his speaking career isn't going to last very long. Be humble and treat everyone you meet with respect and kindness. Here are a few things to keep in mind when you're interacting with conference organizers:

- **Show up early for your gig.** I recommend getting to a venue at least an hour early if possible, to ensure plenty of time to run an A/V check, go to the bathroom, get some water, and get comfortable in the room you're speaking in.

- **Be respectful to the A/V team.** These folks are usually under a lot of pressure to make sure all the technical aspects of a conference go well. Also, I can guarantee they're getting paid a lot less than you are. Be nice to them and don't yell or get angry if there's an issue with the mic, the sound, or your PowerPoint. Trust me, don't piss off the sound team—they can destroy your life if they want to! Take a deep breath and work together to find a solution.

- **Bring everything you need to deliver your talk in your backpack.** As my buddy and CAMPUSPEAK speaker Tim Mousseau, who has delivered hundreds of talks across the country to some 125,000 college students about sexual assault prevention once told me, "You should be show-ready the second you leave your house in the morning." This means, don't expect someone else to have the things you need to hook your laptop up to a projector, and never (ever) put anything you need in a checked bag at the airport. Always carry your own laptop, laptop charger, phone charger, HDMI adapter, VGA adapter, slide clicker, copies of any worksheets or handouts, and a USB thumb drive with several copies of your presentation. Don't expect a venue to have those things for you—they probably will, but they might not.

- **If a conference asks you for your presentation in PowerPoint, give it to them in PowerPoint.** This is a common mistake new speakers make. When I first started speaking, I assumed I would always be able to run my presentation off of my own laptop, in which case I thought I could always use Keynote. I think those of us that are die-hard Mac users can agree that Keynote is better than PowerPoint for simple, design-forward decks. But, I was soon met with the reality that at most talks, you're not allowed to use your own laptop. Have you ever organized a conference before? If you have, you can empathize with the fact that it is a tech efficiency nightmare to have each speaker present off their own laptop. Think about the time it takes for the A/V person to switch out all those laptops, adapters, and cables—it's a disaster.

  Most gigs will want you to submit your presentation two weeks ahead of time, usually in PowerPoint. This is because most conferences are held in shitty old hotel conference rooms and most shitty old hotel conference rooms have shitty old PC computers they run presentations on. My advice is to always make your deck in PowerPoint, not Keynote, and never Prezi or Google Slides. Why not

Keynote? Because most venues don't use Macs. Why not Prezi? Because most conference organizers don't like it when some presenters use Prezi and others don't. Why not Google Slides? Because there's a 97 percent chance the Internet will not be working in the shitty old hotel conference room. Also, unless you are submitting a deck as a PDF, use a standard font on PowerPoint. Why a standard font? Because if you use a super beautiful specialty font you downloaded to your computer, but it's not downloaded on the shitty 2006 PC that the shitty old hotel conference room is using (even though you told the client to download it!), and when you import the new font into PowerPoint and the formatting of your deck is all messed up, and it's only ten minutes before you go on stage, you're going to freak out. In summary: just use PowerPoint. It ain't sexy, but it gets the job done.

- **Dress like you care.** A lot of my millennial friends adopt a casual philosophy when it comes to their speaking appearances. As in, it's cool to wear a t-shirt on stage in front of Fortune 500 executives, because, "I'm like, a millennial, and we're cool and authentic, and I know how to use an iPhone, and I know the best spot in LA for avocado toast and a green juice, and I dress like this every day at home, so why should I dress differently today?" I hear that, but I think if someone is inviting you to speak, or paying for you to fly across the country (or to Europe!), then, yeah, the least you can do is dress like you care. But at the end of the day, you should be comfortable on stage. You do you. But, unless you're Mark Zuckerberg, think twice about wearing ugly-ass running shoes and a wrinkled t-shirt on stage. Here's a good rule of thumb: if you wouldn't wear it for a job interview, then don't wear it on stage. If you're speaking on stage, you should dress a little nicer than the average person in the audience.

- **If you have a book, bring a signed copy for the person who invited you to speak.** It's always a good idea to go out of your way to be generous to the people who are working on your behalf. I always bring a signed copy of my book to gift to the person who booked me to speak (you know, that person you've emailed back-and-forth 24 times with), and one or two extra signed copies for the event team.

- **Treat the greeters, volunteers, and administrative staff well.** I've seen speakers walk into a corporate office and treat the secretary as if they didn't even exist. They act as if the person who invited them to speak was the CEO, and that everyone else who works at the company should kiss their feet. These types of speakers are the worst, and my bet is they don't get booked too often. I'll let you in on a little secret: the people who usually initially recommend speakers to speak at their company are not in the C-suite. Usually, they have titles like "HR specialist" or "employee engagement specialist" or "communications associate," or yes, "executive assistant" or "intern." I once spoke at a company because the executive assistant saw my TED talk and recommended me. Be courteous and respectful to everyone you meet at a company—everyone. You never know who you're speaking to, and you never know if they're the reason you're there in the first place. As my friends at The Unreasonable Institute like to say, "Treat everyone like the messiah."

- **Don't suck.** I once asked a speaker agent with more than 20 years of experience to share his key advice for speakers. "Don't suck," he said. "And be nice to the client. That's pretty much it." I appreciate the brevity. The agent went on to tell me several stories of speakers who did in fact, suck. There was one who got drunk the night before his talk and was clearly out of it on stage. Another who had a breakdown on stage and didn't finish their presentation, and another who yelled at a client. At the end of the day, your job is simple: get on stage, deliver, and don't be a jerk.

# 60

# Master your Q&A

**MY FAVORITE PART OF ANY TALK** is the Q&A. I've done my presentation so many times that it's far more interesting to interact with the audience than it is for me to share my prepared material. However, at this point, I've done my talk so many times, that I usually know what the *questions* are going to be even before the Q&A begins. I love it when someone in the audience asks what they perceive to be a really challenging question about millennials—the 'I'm going to really stump this speaker!' type of question— only to realize that I have prepared detailed and nuanced 500-word essay answers to pretty much any question you could possibly ask me about millennials. This means I've done my homework and I'm good at my job.

Author and public speaker Scott Berkun admits in his excellent tell-all book, *Confessions of a Public Speaker*, which should be required reading for professional speakers, "I've heard your question before… by the third or fourth time I've given a lecture, I've heard 70 percent of the questions I'll likely ever hear on the topic."

Audience Q&A is your opportunity to truly

demonstrate your subject matter expertise, and to connect with the audience. If the audience feels like you aren't able to answer tough questions about your topic, they're going to think you're merely a one-hit wonder who can memorize a talk, not a professional. But if you truly know your stuff, and if you're willing to bring up controversial topics, discussing them in a way that opens up constructive dialogue—which pushes the audience *to ask themselves questions*—then you're going to win over the crowd every time.

Here are a few things you can do to master your Q&A.

1. **Do your research.** Q&A is the perfect time to cite relevant statistics, articles, case studies, and books that are relevant to your keynote. Even better, pointing your audience in the direction of additional resources and reading material shows you care about their learning and growth beyond the speaking engagement.

2. **Make it a conversation.** A great way to make your Q&A more engaging is to start reflecting questions back to the audience. For example, I love asking participants if they can share a personal example of managing millennials in the workplace that was challenging (and one that was successful). First of all, people love sharing their own experiences. Second of all, suddenly now the audience is the expert,

and people love feeling like they're the expert. This creates a dynamic conversation that is a lot more interesting than you answering every single question yourself.

3. **Make it funny.** Q&A is a great place to bring in some humor—and humility to your practice. Admitting that you struggle with some of the same things the audience struggles with, and being able to laugh at yourself goes a long way to making people resonate with you.

4. **If you don't know something, admit it.** If someone asks something that you don't know the answer to, don't make up an answer. Be honest. You can say, "Wow, that's a really interesting question. I haven't considered that before and I honestly can't say I have an answer for you right now. I'd be happy to follow up if you give me your contact info."

5. **Follow up.** Q&A is a perfect time to gauge who in the audience is really ready to dive deeper into your material. If you pay close attention, you can find those people after your presentation. Even better, ask them to say hi, get their business card, and send them an email with a link to other talks you've given, your slides, articles or books you've written, and ways they can engage with your work (or hire

you) moving forward. I've had several clients book me for gigs and when I asked them how they found out about my work, it turned out they were audience members at a previous talk of mine who had asked really poignant questions during Q&A.

# 61

# What to do when shit goes wrong

**I RECENTLY HAD TEA WITH** my friend Chris Ategeka. Chris and I met at the Hive Global Leaders Program a few years ago, where he deejayed one of the best dance parties I've ever been to. This was after Chris (aka DJ Social Impact) gave an inspiring talk about growing up in Uganda after losing both his parents to HIV/AIDS, how he made it to the United States, graduated from UC Berkeley with a master's degree in mechanical engineering, and went on to become a serial entrepreneur, Young Global Leader with the World Economic Forum, Echoing Green fellow, TED fellow, Ashoka Fellow, and *Forbes* 30 Under 30.

Chris founded UCOT, the world's first center for the Unintended Consequences of Technology, and has spoken at the World Economic Forum, Clinton Global Initiative and the United Nations. His recent talk, "How adoption worked for me," delivered on the main stage of TED, was the first talk of 2018 to be featured on TED.com. Yes,

Chris is the coolest dude ever.

Over tea, Chris told me that many TED speakers at the main TED event, which used to be held in Long Beach, California and now is held in Vancouver, Canada, don't ever have their talks put on TED.com. If you don't give a good talk, it's not posted online. I had no idea this was the case. Can you imagine doing something so important that you get invited to speak at TED, telling your whole family you're giving a TED talk, having so many influential people in the audience, practicing your talk for six months straight, and then getting up there and forgetting your whole talk?

What a bummer. I share this because if a TED speaker has a bad day, then you're probably going to bomb at some point as well. I've frozen before. Once, I was giving a talk at a small college in Missouri—I think thirteen people were in the audience—but for whatever reason, I completely lost my train of thought and spaced out. I was like a deer in the headlights—I forgot where I even was. I've given talks in front of thousands of people at very prestigious conferences, and yet I bomb at a tiny college with a few students who had come for the free pizza and Coke?! Classic.

Anyways, I took a deep breath, closed my eyes for a few seconds, and apologized to the students. I said, "I'm sorry, friends, I seem to have gotten so excited about talking about my quarter-life crisis today that I'm having a little quarter-life crisis right now on stage.

Can someone pass me a slice of pizza?" The students smiled, and after taking a sip of water and pausing for a few breaths, I finally remembered where I was, and I continued on with my talk and killed it the rest of the way.

Here are a few tips to help manage worst-case scenarios on stage:

1. **Be real about being nervous.** If you're freaking out before a big talk, let the audience know how nervous you are. Suddenly, they'll be on your side, rooting for you to do a good job. Pro tip: only do this if you're actually nervous. I've seen seasoned speakers be like, "Wow, I'm really nervous up here, I never do this," when clearly they look casual AF, speak all the time, and are just fishing for some audience love. This is a douche move and the audience will sense your bluff right away. Be truly vulnerable. Faking vulnerability (read: lying) is the worst thing you can do.

2. **Remember to breathe.** Almost every speaker I've ever interviewed admits to getting nervous before a gig. Remember: people are more afraid of public speaking than dying. So it makes sense that even veteran speakers get a little anxious before hitting the stage. I recommend the simple but useful practice of doing a little breath work before going on stage. Close your

eyes, and take a few deep breaths. Feel your breath moving throughout the body. If meditation is part of your practice, meditating for 60 seconds (or 10 minutes) before a gig can work wonders. Although, if I'm being honest, sometimes I'm just too amped up for a gig to sit. I sit down to meditate, and before I've even closed my eyes, my heart is racing and I'm pumping my fists in the air. I end up taking a brisk jog around the hotel conference room, not meditating.

3.  **Have a pre-show ritual.** Whatever you do, develop a routine that gets you into the zone before you speak. It might be meditating, or push-ups, or blasting Jay-Z. Here's my routine on the morning of a gig: wake up, go for a 3-mile run, stretch, shower, eat breakfast, drink green tea (I don't like to have coffee before I speak—it makes me too jittery), get dressed (I get dressed after eating—I've spilled oatmeal all over my ironed white dress shirt before—not a good look), and head to the event an hour before start time. A few minutes before going on stage, I blast a pump-up jam in my headphones and have a solo dance party backstage. Then, I'm ready to go.

4.  **Smile.** If something goes wrong, just smile. If the slides stop working, if you forget your lines, if someone in the audience is being rude... remember to smile. Find someone in the audience you know and smile at them.

Don't get mad at anyone—the audience, the A/V folks, or yourself. Chances are, whatever technical problem you're having will get fixed. Once, I was giving a talk at a co-working space in Lisbon and regrettably I got a little aggressive with the audience. About 30-seconds into my presentation, I noticed that everyone was on their laptops as I was speaking— literally the whole room. I was annoyed. I said, "Hey, can all of you put away your laptops? It's really rude." The audience members seemed pissed. One even said, "Well, this is our office. We have work to do, and this is the only place with tables." I said, "Well, you can leave the room if you want to keep working." Big mistake. I had lost the audience before my talk even began. Once you piss off someone in the audience, it's really hard to win them back. I should have just smiled and kept on with my talk. It wasn't the audience's fault—it was the person who booked me and failed to mention that the venue was an active co-working space and people would be working during my presentation.

# Interview with Antonio Neves

"Public speaking isn't for the speaker, it's for the audience."

Antonio Neves is a workplace engagement speaker, author, and award-winning journalist. He has delivered hundreds of keynotes to thousands of people at conferences, top organizations, trade associations, and universities, including Google, NCAA, Starwood Hotels and Resorts, Stanford University, and the American Institute of CPAs. For 10 years, Antonio worked as a television journalist with NBC, PBS, and BET, interviewing top CEOs, entrepreneurs, heads of state, Grammy and Oscar winners. He is the author of *50 Ways to Excel in Your First Job (and in Life)* and his writing has been published in *Inc.* and *Entrepreneur.com*. Antonio has been speaking professionally since 2012, and is paid to speak about 40 times a year, on topics including: millennials in the workplace, workforce engagement, leadership, college success, and the mid-career crisis.

## Why did you start public speaking?

I'm from a small Michigan town. One of those towns that people don't leave. I'm from a blue-collar family. I'm a first-generation college graduate. The first to graduate in my family. I had no idea what was possible in my life. If you told me that I would have gone from my small hometown to earning a masters degree from an Ivy League institution, I would have told you that you are crazy.

I started speaking because I know first-hand the power of belief. What it means when someone believes in you and how that can inspire people to stretch beyond their limits and achieve great things. I started speaking to inspire people to know that they have a choice in their life. That more is possible than they think. I'm a living example of this. I feel like it's my duty to support others and through my words show my belief in them.

## How do you manage to stay so energized when you're on stage?

If you see me before an engagement, I'm quiet and relaxed. Truly, I'm an introvert. Not many people know that about me. However, once I'm introduced, and the "mission" begins, I transform. A light switches on. My awareness is heightened and my background as a journalist starts to come alive. I can read a room even when no one is saying a word. I try to meet people where they are. Most importantly, I work to support them and to be of service. Being of service is the secret. Most speakers just like the attention and that's dicey territory. I truly care about being of service. And most importantly, someone once told me if you don't have fun it doesn't count. So, I do all I can to be well prepared, have fun, be present and give my all.

### How have you marketed your talks?

First, I have never received a booking where someone said, "I saw you on Twitter, Facebook or Instagram." Don't get me wrong, once they find you, they will review your social channels, but I've never been booked because someone saw a tweet of mine.

Early on, the vast majority of my events were booked via a speaking bureau. Today, I'm fortunate to have great organic search results from online searches along with referrals from fellow speakers and past clients. After a talk, a question I always ask a client is, "Is there anyone else in your network, or within your company you know, that I could make a good fit for as a speaker?" That goes far.

## What would be your primary pieces of advice for a new speaker trying to break into the college/corporate speaking market?

Your first job is to be a great speaker. That means studying the art of storytelling and putting in the work. I recommend the books *Steal the Show* by Michael Port and *Confessions of a Public Speaker* by Scott Berkun. Second, watch and learn from great speakers. Next, get gigs under your belt any way that you can. Volunteer, do them for free, whatever it takes. Fourth, find a mentor, someone that can guide you and provide advice. The best way to get a mentor is to treat someone like they are your mentor. Not to directly ask, "Will you be my mentor?" Fifth, regularly hit record. Record your talks. Create content and press publish. It may not be great initially, but it builds confidence and a track record.

## Anything else you want to share?

If you decide to pursue public speaking, do it for the right reasons. Most do it for validation. To feel of value. To feel important. To say, "look at me!" In many ways, public speaking isn't for the speaker, it's for the audience. How speakers can support them. Never take a talk for granted. Never "wing it." Winging it is easy when you're well prepared. Learn what your client wants so you can meet their needs. Ask them what success looks like. Give more than you take.

**Connect with Antonio:** theantonioneves.com,
@theantonioneves

# 62

# If only one person shows up, that's a life you can change

**AS YOU BUILD YOUR** speaking career, you will sometimes find yourself speaking in front of a packed house. There is nothing more exhilarating than speaking to several hundred—or several thousand people—all of those people paying attention to your every word. Talk about a dopamine rush! Public speaking is more fun than any drug I've done in my life.

However, you'll also likely find yourself in front of much smaller crowds. Sometimes you may even have to deliver a talk in front of just a few people. Have you ever traveled across the country for a gig, had two delayed flights, gotten just three hours of sleep, only to show up to a room of only five people? It happens all the time to professional speakers.

Recently, I went to see my buddy Jeff Kirschner give a talk at The Battery, an invite-only social club in San

Francisco. I mentioned Jeff in Part One, he runs Litterati, a global community dedicated to eradicating litter one piece at a time. Jeff has spoken at TED, Google, and MIT, so he's no stranger to speaking to large crowds. However, when he showed up at The Battery for a 7:30pm talk on a Thursday night, the only people there were me and Jeff's friend Chas. Sadly, I think there was a Golden State Warriors playoff game happening the same night, and let's just say people in the Bay Area love the Dubs—just a tad more than they like picking up litter.

Jeff told me that once he spoke at an Earth Day event where the organizer had told him 600 people would be in the audience, and when he showed up, there were only seven people. "All I need is one," Jeff said. "If one person shows up, that's one more person that might be inspired to make a difference."

I respect Jeff's attitude. Ten people ended up attending Jeff's Battery talk, and the crowd was left inspired and eager to take more responsibility in their personal relationship to litter and reducing waste in their community. Three or four of the attendees gave Jeff their business card after his presentation, which means warm leads for future paid speaking gigs.

Treat every single person in the audience with respect. I once did an unpaid talk at a top consulting firm in New York in front of four people. I felt like a loser. One year later, a woman came up to me at a leadership conference I was emceeing. I had no idea who she was, but she was one of the four people in the audience that day. Apparently, my talk had inspired her to make the career transition from a depressed management consultant to a job she loved in impact investing.

Small talks are often even more impactful for audience members, because they have a more intimate relationship with the speaker. It can be a great opportunity for you to engage participants in your talk, spend more time meeting people, and do a small group discussion or Q&A.

If just one person shows up, that's someone who cares about what you have to say, and that's a life you can change. No one cares how many Instagram followers you have. All that matters is that you inspire your audience.

# 63

# Relationship building is everything

**EARLIER, I TOLD THE STORY** of how speaking at my friend Hung's conference on company culture, Culture Summit, led to me booking a lucrative gig at MailChimp (in addition to another well-paid gig at Salesforce and speaking leads at several other companies). But I forget to mention how Hung and I met in the first place. In early 2015, I received an email from Hung that said:

Hey Smiley,

I just finished your book and it was such a great book. It validated so many things I've been feeling the last six years, I wish I had found it sooner (I'm 35 now). Just wanted to let you know that I'm living my purpose by producing a conference called Culture Summit on June 26.

If you're around then, you should come by and check it out. Would love to connect.

I went to check out Hung's event and we kept in touch. I gave Hung some advice for self-publishing his own book about overcoming depression and how the experience shaped his journey. Not long after that, Hung emailed me:

**Would love to have you speak next year, Smiley! Something about millennials (how to manage, keep them engaged, etc.). I'll make sure to follow up with you for the next one.**

That led to me speaking at Culture Summit 2016 (for free)—the gig where MailChimp was in the room, and then emcee'ing Culture Summit 2017 (also for free). In fact, I just had lunch with Hung, and he invited me to emcee Culture Summit again in 2018, and this time he's paying me some money.

I share this to illustrate a few things about booking speaking gigs:

1. **Play the long game.** Relationship building takes time. It was more than a year between the time Hung and I met and the time he invited me to speak at his event. It will be almost *three years* between the time we met and the time Hung pays me for a gig (but in that time, he has also indirectly helped me earn tens of thousands of dollars).

2. **Be grateful.** The reason Hung and I met was because he liked my book. He was appreciative of the time I spent sharing my story. In return, I was appreciative that Hung had told me how much the book had meant to him. Gratitude is the essence of any relationship worth investing in.

3. **Give and it will come back to you.** As Wharton professor and author Adam Grant proves in his book *Give and Take*, people get farther in business (and in life) when they offer their gifts to their network and help others. I offered my book-writing advice to Hung without expecting anything in return, and eventually it came back to help me too.

# 64

# The power of referrals and repeat bookings

**A GIG ISN'T OVER WHEN** you walk off the stage. It's over after you've thanked the client and ensured they're satisfied with your performance. If they are, excellent! If not, learn what you could have done better. Most importantly, if a client and their colleagues enjoyed your talk, you want to capture this with a testimonial from the person who booked you or from other audience members. These testimonials are crucial marketing assets for you. My friend Jaymin Patel, who speaks about the power of networking, goes even one step further: he gets video testimonials from his client using his iPhone. Social proof goes a long way.

Furthermore, always ask the client if they can introduce you to two or three other people who might be interested in your talk. The majority of my gigs have been booked through word-of-mouth referrals and from people who have seen me speak and then recommended me.

Another key source of revenue for professional speakers is repeat bookings. Several top speakers on CAMPUSPEAK's roster told me that they entered each academic year knowing that they had at least 10 gigs, even if they weren't formalized yet, that were all universities they had spoken at previously. That's a solid revenue stream from which to build your speaking business. As James Robilotta, a top college leadership speaker, shares:

**"In the frequently inconsistent speaking business, repeat bookings are coveted. When speaking to colleges, there are three main ways to get repeat customers. The first way is to have a speech that is geared towards a population that changes annually. For example, first year students, new members of fraternities and sororities, commencements (though these are hard to come by). The second way is to sell your services to a campus as a multi-talk package…The last way to get repeat business is to sell your speech as a multi-year package. So, you would say, 'For $8000, I will be your new student orientation speaker for the next three years.' Every institution is different. I find it's always best to show up and kill a speech there first before you start to offer them packages. Prove your worth to them and, more importantly, your ability to connect and care for their students."**

One way to ensure you gain more repeat bookings is to keep your talks as interactive as possible. It's hard to get invited back to give the same keynote to the same audience—once they've seen it, they've seen it. But if your talk is more of an experiential workshop, it will be fresh and new every single time. I mentioned that Tom Chi has been invited to give his rapid prototyping workshop at the Hive Global Leaders Program, a conference I used to emcee, more than ten times. Adam Rosendahl from LATE NITE ART has also presented at Hive half a dozen times. Tom and Adam are able to do this because their content relies on audience participation and co-creation; their talks are far more interesting than one person standing on stage and clicking through a PowerPoint.

Think of how sweet it is to have a client that brings you multiple gigs; this means that from just one 30-minute sales call, you can potentially book multiple gigs, and earn tens of thousands of dollars of revenue.

# 65

# Get rejected

**AS YOU BUILD YOUR** speaking business, chances are you'll get rejected from many of the opportunities you apply for. Good. Getting rejected means you're putting yourself out there and building future relationships. Just to give a personal plug for rejection: in the past two years, I've been rejected by TED three times. I was rejected from the TED Idea Search—in which thousands of people submit a 1-minute video submission, and around 10 people are selected to give a TED talk at the TED offices in New York City, and of those people, the best is selected to give a talk on the main stage at TED in Vancouver. It's a long shot, but I think every speaker should apply to the TED Idea Search every year for practice.

I've also been rejected from the TED Residency—two years in a row. I consider these rejections small wins that have allowed me to practice honing my message and filming short 1-minute videos. It might not happen next year, or in five years, or even in ten years, but one of these days, I'm going to make it onto to that TED main stage, and it'll be because of all the rejections I had along the way.

Here's another example of why rejection is positive. A speaker friend of mine was recently told that he was going to give the opening keynote in front of several thousand student leaders, at one of the largest and most prestigious college leadership conferences in the country. Can you imagine how excited he was? But, a few weeks before the conference he received a call letting him know that he had been bumped from the keynote—for Joe Biden. My friend was obviously bummed, but how bummed can you really be if the person you're losing a gig to is Joe Biden? My buddy still got to speak at the conference and I'm sure that rejection story will keep pushing him for years to come.

# 66

# Get your friends on stage

**I ONCE HAD A FRIEND GET UPSET** at me for sharing a conference call for speakers on my Facebook page because she was applying to the conference, and she didn't want too many other people to apply. This selfish approach might get you a gig or two, but it will not help you build a sustainable speaking career.

It's far better to build relationships with other speakers, especially speakers who speak about the same topic as you. Why? Whenever I'm offered a gig that I'm unavailable for, who do you think I recommend? My speaker friends who have offered me gigs, nominated me for gigs, or given me helpful advice. Most speakers are booked on referral, so you want to be someone who has added value for other speakers and conference organizers. When a conference reaches out to me to speak, whether I'm available for the gig or not, I always ask them if I can recommend a few other speakers for their event. This way I get to help speakers in my network (and make sure my friends and I get to hang out in really cool places all around the world!).

The more you speak, the more leverage you gain to help others in your community. For example, a few years ago, I spoke at a digital innovation and start-up festival called Year of the X in Munich, Germany. The audience really enjoyed my presentation on The Future of Work, and I stayed in touch with the conference organizer of the conference, Markus von der Lühe, after the event. The next year, I sent him an email recommending ten speakers—all women—for Year of the X. He ended up booking five of them. The year after that, he invited me back to Munich and I again recommended about a dozen women speakers in my network—several of whom got the gig. Not only that, but the women I recommended were then able to recommend speakers in their own networks. Obviously, not everyone you recommend is going to be a fit for every event, but you can always try to pay it forward.

My friend Dr. Emily Anhalt has a doctorate in clinical psychology and she speaks about emotional fitness and mental health, helping high-growth tech companies invest in their employees by tackling common issues such as burnout, communication and collaboration challenges, and imposter syndrome. She recently tweeted her brilliant thoughts on supporting the success of others:

"One sign of an Emotionally Fit leader is a genuine desire to foster collaboration instead of competition, and to elevate others personally and professionally. This can be easier said than done, and I have thoughts about why that is: I believe that somewhere deep down, we all fear that there isn't enough success to go around. That success is a pie, and every time someone gets a slice, there's less left for the rest of us. That we must protect our wisdom, time, and mind, lest it be stolen for another's gain.

Envy in its extreme form is the desire to destroy something you don't have to avoid the discomfort of not having it. This is why we secretly hope others will fail—not because we don't want their success, but because their success puts us in touch with our own feelings of failure.

I have found this to be especially true with women, perhaps because it really can feel like there is less for us. The frequency with which I see women holding each other down instead of lifting each other up astounds me (not that I am innocent of such behavior). But what if instead, we all trusted that as we elevate others, we will be carried up with them? That seeds of empathy and altruism we plant now will grow tenfold into dividends we never could have predicted? That no one gets to the top alone? Start by giving a shout-out to someone who has helped you get to where you are today. Someone who has your back and genuinely wants you to succeed."

Remember my friend who was upset that I posted the call

for speakers on Facebook? Well, guess what? She didn't get the gig—a friend of hers did. But that friend recommended her for the conference the following year.

Approach your speaking business with an abundance mindset rather than a scarcity mindset. There are hundreds of conferences and speaking opportunities all around the world, every single day of the year. When one person succeeds, you do too. When you look back on your speaking career, you will measure your success based on how many other people you helped get gigs, not how many gigs you had. As my dear friend Evan Kleiman likes to say, "We're all in this together."

# 67

# Remember to take care of yourself

**AS YOU BUILD YOUR** speaking career, never forget to take care of yourself and remember what matters most. The life of a Breakthrough Speaker can be grueling and lonely at times. Sure, you're traveling around the country, and sometimes you get to travel to exotic locations, but the majority of days are spent traveling in between gigs, on airplanes, in hotel rooms, in rental cars and Ubers, often alone. It's easy to start to feel like George Clooney in *Up in the Air*.

One of my speaking mentors, Tim Mousseau, recommends a blog post titled, "Letting Go of a Dream: Why I Left Professional Speaking," written by a successful professional speaker named Jason Connell. In the post, Jason recounts the emotional toll that speaking took on his life, and how hard it was to live on the road and be away 200 days a year from friends, family, and his partner.

When you're doing something you love that requires intense physical exertion, the risk of burnout is high. There have been times where I was eating dinner all by myself at

10pm in a hotel bar in suburban Phoenix, thinking, 'This can't be my life. I don't want to live like this.' Remember to prioritize balance and rest. I obviously hope you make as much money as possible from speaking, but I think once people start chasing overly-ambitious financial and professional goals, they become overwhelmed and miserable—they work too hard, forget who they are, forget to care for themselves, and forget what really matters.

To fight loneliness and travel fatigue whenever possible, make your speaking business about something more than just speaking. Build leisure into your practice. Spend time with friends and family while you're on the road. Invite a partner or best friend along with you for a conference. Extend your travel to visit an old friend. Explore the city you're visiting. Go for an adventure, or explore somewhere you've never been before. Relax in nature. Do creative activities you love. Treat yourself to time off. Get recommendations for delicious local restaurants. Eat healthy and fresh food whenever possible, and incorporate daily exercise into your routine, which can be challenging when you travel.

Most importantly, always remember why you started speaking in the first place. Come back to your why, your personal story, and the message you want to share with the world. Read a few emails that people have sent you, sharing what your talk meant to them and how it changed their life. This will keep you energized when you feel depleted. And if you get really exhausted, don't feel ashamed, take a break from the road and spend more time with the people you love most.

# 68

# Keep going

**ONCE YOU START SPEAKING,** life will take you to some unexpected places. Some of these moments may be truly beautiful, and some may be incredibly difficult. I'm reminded of the words of my friend Kristin Hayden, who recently gave a TEDx talk in Himi, Japan called "Everything starts with a vision." Kristin is a social entrepreneur, public speaker, Ashoka fellow, co-founder of VisionVenture, and chief partnership officer at IGNITE, an organization that's building a national movement to inspire young women to run for public office. "I wish that someone had told me to hold the vision, but let go of how it looks," Kristin shares. "We never get there how we think we're gonna get there, so we should just let go of that. But if we stay committed to what we want to create in life, we will get there, but it will be—probably—in very unexpected ways."

After a year or two or five, you may get to a point where you grow tired of your keynote. You'll think to yourself, "Oh my fucking god, if I have to stand on stage and tell my rehearsed story with the Tinder joke one more time, I'm going to lose my mind." There's a point where it's no longer fun to be a one-hit wonder—even if you're getting paid very well to be a one-hit wonder. Now you know how Chumbawamba feels.

When that happens, it's time to pause and find something new to speak about. Write a new book, make something beautiful, launch a new product, build a movement, find partners to collaborate with, work for an organization or a cause you care about, or take a vacation to reflect on what you want. This isn't cheating on your speaking practice, it's giving it fuel. Creating a new anchor will give you something new to speak about. This is exactly what I did recently. I started to get a little tired of speaking about millennials, so this year I spent less time on the road speaking and more time writing this book about public speaking, and working on a new book about the importance of friendship in the digital age.

The best thing about sharing your story for a living is that it's your story, and you can always edit it as you go.

Before we close, I want to share a short story about my friend Matthew Wetschler's unusual journey into public speaking. Matt is an emergency medicine doctor, artist, and surfer. We became friends when he had finished his medical residency at Stanford University, and was living in the Bay Area. A week before Thanksgiving 2017, Matt was body surfing at Ocean Beach in San Francisco, and a strong wave crashed him head first into the ocean floor, breaking his neck. Matt was unconscious for several minutes, floating in the water like a piece of garbage. He recalls, "As I took my last breath, I screamed into the water... I knew I was going to die."

Matt was very lucky. He doesn't know how long he was without breath in the water, but another surfer dragged his body to the shore and two people that day on the beach happened to have medical training. One was an ICU nurse, who gave him CPR, and the other was a physician. Matt was rushed to Zuckerberg San Francisco General Hospital, and began a miraculous path to recovery. Assuming at first that he wouldn't be able to walk ever again because of his traumatic spinal cord injury, six months later, Matt is now walking again. Furthermore, he has renewed his passion for art, painting, and drawing the entire time he was in rehab— even at times when he couldn't feel any movement in his hand.

In December, I visited Matt when he was in the spinal cord injury rehabilitation unit of Santa Clara Valley Medical Center (interestingly enough, the same hospital where Matt had done part-time work as an emergency room doctor). Despite being in a wheelchair and barely able to put food in his mouth, Matt had turned his hospital room into an art studio. Matt told me that the accident had given him a fresh outlook on life. He was less worried about career advancement and "success," and a lot more focused on being able to lift a little more weight each day with his hands, on being able to take a sip of water without help, and creating art. He had learned to find joy in the simple things.

In May 2018, six months after his accident, I attended Matt's art opening at the Great Highway Gallery in the Outer Sunset, just a few blocks from where he had been body surfing. The gallery was packed with Matt's friends and family admiring the brilliant work he had created while recovering from his spinal cord injury. So many people were there that you had to wait to get inside. Matt was walking around, without a wheelchair or a cane, drinking a beer, schmoozing everyone up, trying to get people to bid more money on his paintings.

Just the other day, I received a text message from Matt that made me smile: "Smiley, I just locked down my first paid speaking gig! I'm excited and feeling energized to make a really tight presentation." Matt is going to be speaking at a company retreat on overcoming adversity and creative potential.

I share Matt's story to remind you to keep going. To prove that wherever life takes us, however unexpected our path becomes, there's always a lesson, there's always a silver lining, there's always a ray of light in a sea of darkness. Your story is always worth sharing. You get to write (and re-write) your own narrative, and we need you to, because there are other people out there who need to hear it now.

The journey to becoming a Breakthrough Speaker is not easy, but it is so worth it. Breakthrough Speakers bring people to action. How else are we going to solve the grave challenges facing our generation—and our children's generation? As the saying goes, "Your truth will set us free." As you speak your truth, share your truth, and get paid for your truth, I know you'll be empowering others to do the same.

I can't wait to see you on stage.

# Resources

For an updated list of resources, check out *smileyposwolsky.com/thebreakthroughspeaker*.

**Books about public speaking**
*TED Talks* by Chris Anderson
*Talk Like TED* by Carmine Gallo
*Confessions of a Public Speaker* by Scott Berkun
*Steal the Show* by Michael Port

**Books about storytelling, communications, and personal branding**
*Your Story is Your Power* by Elle Luna and Susie Herrick
*Stand Out* and *Entrepreneurial You* by Dorie Clark
*The Faraway Nearby* by Rebecca Solnit
*The Storyteller's Secret* by Carmine Gallo
*The Hero with a Thousand Faces* by Joseph Campbell
*Made to Stick* by Chip Heath and Dan Heath
*Perennial Seller* by Ryan Holiday

**Books about the creative process**
*Bird by Bird* by Anne Lamott
*The Artist's Way* by Julia Cameron
*Big Magic* by Elizabeth Gilbert
*The War of Art* by Steven Pressfield
*Draft No. 4* by John McPhee

## Books about things that matter
*Feminist Fight Club* by Jessica Bennett
*You Can't Touch My Hair* by Phoebe Robinson
*Reset* by Ellen Pao
*The Art of Gathering* by Priya Parker
*Daring Greatly* by Brené Brown
*Tiny Beautiful Things* by Cheryl Strayed

## Speaker agencies
FRESH Speakers
CAMPUSPEAK
SpeakInc
Washington Speakers Bureau
The Harry Walker Agency
The Lavin Agency Speakers Bureau
Worldwide Speakers Group
Executive Speakers
Premiere Speakers Bureau
Eagles Talent Speakers Bureau
Goodman Speakers Bureau
Keppler Speakers
Promenade Speakers
The Speakers Agency
Global Speakers Agency
WSB Direct Connect
eSpeakers (speaker directory)

**Podcasts**

The Speaker Lab with Grant Baldwin

Steal the Show with Michael Port

Call Your Girlfriend with Aminatou Sow and Ann Friedman

2 Dope Queens with Jessica Williams and Phoebe Robinson

On Being with Krista Tippett

#SECURETHESEAT with Minda Harts

Startup Pregnant with Sarah K Peck

Gutted Stories with Allie Stark

Heroine with Majo Molfino

Ear Hustle

How I Built This

Trailblazers.FM

The Moth

99% Invisible

Radiolab

This American Life

## Lists of Women and POC Speakers

**Female Tech Speakers**

*femaletechspeakers.com*

A list of women speakers in tech.

**List of 1000 Tech and Science Speakers Who Aren't Cis Men**

*mic.com/articles/175136/women-in-tech-1000-names-no-*

*more-all-male-panels-conferences*
A list of 1000 women speakers from Mic reporter Melanie Ehrenkranz.

## List of 200 Women Influencers in Crypto & Blockchain
medium.com/@michelletsng/201-thought-leaders-in-crypto-and-blockchain-the-ultimate-crypto-list-for-event-planners-9e712186cbfb
This list curated by Michelle Tsng will help you find a speaker for your next panel on blockchain or crypto.

## More Women's Voices
*morewomensvoices.com*
A list of women entrepreneurs, business owners, authors, podcast hosts, and speakers curated by Sarah K Peck.

## The Women Speaker Initiative
*smileyposwolsky.com/womenspeakerinitiative*
A list of women and POC speakers from The Women Speaker Initiative.

## Networks and Speaker Diversity

## 50/50 Pledge
*5050pledge.com*
Works to showcase an equal share of men's and women's voices at the top technology industry conferences. Join

their private directory of professional women in tech!

## Dreamers/Doers

*dreamersdoers.me*

A high-impact membership community of trailblazing, entrepreneurial women.

## FRESH Speakers

*freshspeakers.com*

A speaking agency representing a diverse range of new voices.

## Ladies Get Paid

*ladiesgetpaid.com*

Women's professional development organization working to close the gender wage and leadership gap, with 20,000 members and 18 chapters across the country. Provides education, resources and community for women to advance at work.

## Lesbians Who Tech

*lesbianswhotech.org*

A community of queer women in and around tech.

## Owen Pledge

*owen.org/pledge*

Pledge to not be a part of all-male panels.

## Speaker Diversity

*speakerdiversity.com*

Pledge to not be a part of all-male panels.

## Stilobox

*stilobox.com*

A resource for aspiring women leaders to speak more. Every week, Stilobox shares speaking opportunities, stories of inspirational female leaders, and events focused on empowering women.

## Tech Inclusion

*techinclusion.co*

Exploring innovative solutions to tech diversity and inclusion.

## Tech Ladies

*hiretechladies.com*

A job board and community for women in tech.

## The Female Quotient

*thefemalequotient.com*

The Female Quotient is committed to advancing equality in the workplace. The Girls' Lounge brings women together through experiences to activate change at conferences, corporations, and college campuses.

## The Margin
*themargin.co*
The Margin makes space for people of color at gatherings everywhere.

## The Women Speaker Initiative Facebook Group
*facebook.com/groups/255406128253292*
Private Facebook group for speakers in The Women Speaker Initiative. Please join!

## #Upfront
*weareupfront.com*
Making stages around the world more diverse and accessible, by inviting audience members to share the stage during a keynote.

## Women Catalysts
*womencatalysts.com*
Events and membership organization that hosts talks and workshops where you can connect with other women on a mission.

# The Women Speaker Initiative

The Women Speaker Initiative aims to increase the number of women and people of color speaking at conferences and companies, as well as ensure that underrepresented speakers are paid competitively as compared to their colleagues.

The Women Speaker Initiative achieves this by connecting professional or aspiring speakers (specifically women and people of color) with other speakers, so that they can share resources and guidance with each other about: how to book more gigs and gain more speaking experience, how to negotiate higher speaking fees, and how to price your talks competitively in an industry where women/POC are consistently underpaid.

Interested in participating in this initiative? Please join our directory and Facebook group of more than 1,000 speakers. It is free to participate. *Anyone* who is dedicated to empowering women and POC in the speaking industry is welcome.

100 percent of the profits from sales of this book will go toward supporting efforts of The Women Speaker Initiative.

Learn more: *smileyposwolsky.com/womenspeakerinitiaitve*

# Bonus Gift

In order to help your speaking career, I've created several free bonus materials. Go to *smileyposwolsky.com/thebreak-throughspeaker* to receive your gift:

- 10 full-length interviews with Breakthrough Speakers featured in the book
- An updated Breakthrough Speaker Resources Guide

**Spread the word**

If you found this book useful, please share it with your friends and community, as a way of spreading the love and encouraging your peers to find their voice. There are a number of easy ways to do this:

1. Write an Amazon review of the book.
2. Gift this book to a friend or stranger who needs to read it.
3. Instagram a selfie of you reading the book (#Break-throughSpeaker).
4. Write a blog post about building your speaking career.
5. Host a #BreakthroughSpeaker-themed dinner party at your house and talk about how your friends can support each other's speaking careers.

# Breakthrough Speakers

**(In order of appearance)**

**Debbie Sterling**
goldieblox.com

**Ted Gonder**
tedgonder.com

**Tom D'Eri**
risingtidecarwash.
com/tom-deri

**Emma Gonzalez**
twitter.com/
Emma4Change
marchforourlives.com

**Minda Harts**
mindaharts.com

**Robin
Farmanfarmaian**
thepatientceo.com

**Ashanti Branch**
everforwardclub.org

**Hana Nobel**
hananobel.com

**Erika Barraza**
erikabarraza.com

**Bryan Stevenson**
bryanstevenson.com
eji.org

**Dawn J. Fraser**
dawnjfraser.com

**Cloe Shasha**
twitter.com/cloe_
shasha
about.me/cloeshasha

**Meltem Demirors**
twitter.com/Melt_Dem

**Elle Luna**
instagram.com/
elleluna
elleluna.com

**Julie Lythcott-Haims**
julielythcotthaims.com

**Chelsea Rustrum**
rustrum.com

**Cam Adair**
camerondare.com

**Kat Alexander**
katalexander.com

**Jeff Kirschner**
litterati.org

**Tristan Harris**
tristanharris.com
humanetech.com

**Amy Lazarus**
inclusionventures.com

**Justin Rosenstein**
en.wikipedia.org/wiki/
Justin_Rosenstein

**Lisa Lee**
linkedin.com/in/
misslisalee

**Lauren Burke**
theposslab.com

**Tiffany Yu**
tiffanyyu.com

**Nikita Mitchell**
nikitatmitchell.com

**Richie Etwaru**
linkedin.com/in/
richieetwaru

**Haben Girma**
habengirma.com

**Molly Sonsteng**

mollysonsteng.com

**Josh Linkler**

joshlinkner.com

**Monica Kang**

linkedin.com/in/
monicakang
innovatorsbox.com

**Saya Iwasaki**

sayaiwasaki.com

**Sarah K Peck**

sarahkpeck.com

**John Henry**

instagram.com/
johnhenrystyle
harlem.capital

**Goldie Chan**

linkedin.com/in/goldie

**Max Stossel**

maxstossel.com

**Tim Mousseau**

timmousseau.com

**Jordan Axani**

jordanaxani.com

**Larissa May**

instagram.com/
livinlikelarz
halfthestoryproject.
com

**Adam Rosendahl**

lateniteart.com

**Tom Chi**

tomchi.com

**Torin Perez**

torinperez.com

**Shira Abramowitz**

shiraabramowitz.com

**Jenny Sauer-Klein**

jennysauerklein.com

**Duleesha Kulasooriya**
linkedin.com/in/
duleeshakulasooriya

**Antonio Neves**
theantonioneves.com

**Michelle Kim**
michellekimconsulting.
com

**Avery Blank**
averyblank.com

**Vanessa Shaw**
humansideoftech.com

**Charlotte Raybourn**
charlotteraybourn.com

**Dorie Clark**
dorieclark.com

**Nate Bagley**
loveumentary.com

**Dan Ram**
iamdanram.com

**Scott Berkun**
scottberkun.com

**Chris Ategeka**
christopherategeka.
com

**Jaymin Patel**
jayminspeaks.com

**James Robilotta**
jamestrobo.com

**Dr. Emily Anhalt**
dremilyanhalt.com

**Kristin Hayden**
linkedin.com/in/
kristinyhayden
thevisionconversation.
com

**Matthew Wetschler**
matthewwetschler.
com

# Notes

## Introduction

*In 2016, in the U.S. alone, the meetings industry...*
Loren G. Edelstein, "U.S. Meetings Industry Generated $845 Billion in Business Sales in 2016, Per New Research," Meetings & Conventions, February 21, 2018, http://www.meetings-conventions.com/News/Industry-Associations/U-S--Meetings-Industry-economic-statistics-$845-Billion-in-Business-Sales-in-2016/.

*Every day, 1.5 million TED talks*
Carmine Gallo. *Talk Like TED* (New York: St. Martin's Press, 2014), 4.

*Every single minute, 300 hours of video*
Nicole Dieker, "Infographic: The Absolutely Ridiculous Amount of Content Consumed Every Minute," *Contently*, July 26, 2016, http://contently.com/strategist/2016/07/26/infographic-content-consumed-every-minute-absolutely-ridiculous/.

*Recent article in The Atlantic*
Ed Yong, "Women Are Invited to Give Fewer Talks Then Men at Top U.S. Universities," *The Atlantic*, December 18, 2017, http://www.theatlantic.com/science/archive/2017/12/women-are-invited-to-give-fewer-talks-than-men-at-top-us-universities/548657/.

*Forbes did an expose on the pay gap*
Christina Wallace, "It's Time To End The Pay Gap For Speakers At Tech Conferences," *Forbes*, March 13, 2017, http://www.forbes.com/sites/christinawallace/2017/03/13/pay-gap-for-speakers-at-tech-conferences/.

*Mic ran a popular article*
Melanie Ehrenkranz, "Think there aren't qualified women in tech? Here are 1,000 names. No more excuses," *Mic*, May 2, 2017, http://mic.com/articles/175136/women-in-tech-1000-names-no-more-all-male-panels-conferences.

*Emma Gonzalez speech*
Emma Gonzalez, "Florida student to NRA and Trump: 'We call BS'," YouTube video, Published by CNN, February 17, 2018, http://www.youtube.com/watch?v=ZxD3o-9H1lY.

*1 in 5 C-Suite leaders is a woman, that just 1 in 30 is a woman of color*
Time's Up Website, Source data: LeanIn.org and McKinsey & Company, "Women in the Workplace," 2017, Retrieved May 31, 2018, http://www.timesupnow.com/.

*Currently only 4 black CEOs in the Fortune 500*
Gillian B. White, "There Are Currently 4 Black CEOs in the Fortune 500," *The Atlantic*, October 26, 2017, http://www.theatlantic.com/business/archive/2017/10/black-ceos-fortune-500/543960/.

*White non-Hispanic women are paid 81 cents on the dollar…*
Time's Up Website, Source data: Economic Policy Institute, Retrieved May 31, 2018, http://www.timesupnow.com/.

*Billionaire investor Warren Buffet…*
Carmine Gallo, "Billionaire Warren Buffet Says This 1 Skill Will Boost Your Career Value by 50 percent," *Inc.*, January 5, 2017, http://www.inc.com/carmine-gallo/the-one-skill-warren-buffett-says-will-raise-your-value-by-50.html.

## Part I

## Why We Speak

*As [Robin] says in one of her talks*
Robin Farmanfarmaian, "DHD16 - Day 1 - Robin Farmanfarmaian, ARC," YouTube Video, http://thepatientceo.com/, Retrieved on June 3, 2018.

## What's Your Story?

*In The Faraway Nearby*
Rebecca Solnit. *The Faraway Nearby* (New York: Viking, 2013), 3.

*"Your goal is not to be Winston Churchill"*
Chris Anderson. *TED Talks* (New York: Mariner Books, 2016), 10.

## Connect, educate, inspire, endure

*Stevenson tells harsh truths about the criminal justice system*
Bryan Stevenson, "Bryan Stevenson: We need to talk about an injustice," TED video, TED.com, March 2012, http://www.ted.com/talks/bryan_stevenson_we_

need_to_talk_about_an_injustice.

*In Bryan Stevenson's words*
Bryan Stevenson, "Bryan Stevenson: We need to talk about an injustice," TED video, TED.com, March 2012, http://www.ted.com/talks/bryan_stevenson_we_need_to_talk_about_an_injustice.

*After Stevenson's talk, the TED community ended up donating $1.3 million*
Chris Anderson. *TED Talks* (New York: Mariner Books, 2016), 24.

*Stevenson almost never even went to TED*
Carmine Gallo. Talk Like TED (New York: St. Martin's Press, 2014), 42.

**Part II**

**The audience is your classroom**

*Chris Anderson shares how one time a TED speaker spent the majority of his talk*
Chris Anderson. *TED Talks* (New York: Mariner Books, 2016), 22-23.

**Make it interactive**

*LinkedIn founder and CEO Reid Hoffman writes*
Reid Hoffman, "Why panels suck," LinkedIn, June 19, 2017, http://www.linkedin.com/pulse/why-panels-suck-reid-hoffman/.

*Professor of Psychology Jean Twenge from San Diego State University notes*
Jean Twenge, "With teen mental health deteriorating over five years, there's a likely culprit," The Conversation, November 14, 2017, http://theconversation.com/with-teen-mental-health-deteriorating-over-five-years-theres-a-likely-culprit-86996.

*Half the Story was recently named one of CNN's*
Sara Ashley O'Brien and Kaya Yurieff, 7 startups that want to improve your mental health," CNN Money, May 25, 2018, http://money.cnn.com/gallery/technology/2018/05/25/self-care-apps-mental-health/7.html.

**Prepare for the future of conferences and experience design**

*Study by Harris Group…*

Uptin Saiidi, "Millennials are prioritizing 'experiences' over stuff," CNBC, May 5, 2016, http://www.cnbc.com/2016/05/05/millennials-are-prioritizing-experiences-over-stuff.html.

*Airbnb Experiences… grew 12x…*
Leigh Gallagher, "Airbnb CEO: Here's How 'Experiences' Are Doing So Far," *Fortune*, October 23, 2017, http://fortune.com/2017/10/23/airbnb-ceo-experiences-new-york/.

**Part III**

**A rant on conferences that only book white dudes to speak**

*One study found that men gave more than twice as many talks*
Ed Yong, "Women Are Invited to Give Fewer Talks Then Men at Top U.S. Universities," *The Atlantic*, December 18, 2017, http://www.theatlantic.com/science/archive/2017/12/women-are-invited-to-give-fewer-talks-than-men-at-top-us-universities/548657/.

*A University of California Hastings study, based on interviews of 60 women of color in STEM fields*
Shalene Gupta, "Study: 100% of women in STEM experience bias," *Fortune*, January 26, 2015, http://fortune.com/2015/01/26/study-100-of-women-of-color-in-stem-experience-bias/.

*Dorie Clark… breaks down the following speaking fee ranges*
Dorie Clark, "How Much Should You Charge for a Speech?," *Harvard Business Review*, May 3, 2018, https://hbr.org/2018/05/how-much-should-you-charge-for-a-speech.

*Here are speaking fees…*
Please note, speaking fees are variable and the fees referenced may not be accurate. They were cited from the following industry websites:

> Thayla Thwarp: Executive Speakers Website, http://www.executivespeakers.com/speaker/Twyla_Tharp/, Retrieved on June 1, 2018.
> Brené Brown: Executive Speakers Website, http://www.executivespeakers.com/speaker/Brene_Brown, Retrieved on May 30, 2018.
> Gary Vaynerchuk: Speaking.com Website, http://speaking.com/speakers/gary-vaynerchuk/, Retrieved on May 30, 2018.
> Barack Obama: Steven W Thrasher, "Barack Obama's $400,000 speaking fees reveal what few want to admit," *The Guardian*, May 1, 2017,

http://www.theguardian.com/commentisfree/2017/may/01/barack-obama-speaking-fees-economic-racial-justice.


## What should you get out of an unpaid gig?

*Avery Blank...likes to say*
Avery Blank, "5 Things To Ask For When You Are Not Getting Paid To Speak," *Forbes*, March 6, 2018, http://www.forbes.com/sites/averyblank/2018/03/06/5-things-to-ask-for-when-you-are-not-getting-paid-to-speak/.


## Remember to take care of yourself

*Blog post titled, "Letting Go of a Dream: Why I Left Professional Speaking"*
Jason Connell, "Letting Go of a Dream: Why I Left Professional Speaking," Jason Connell, October 3, 2016, http://jasonconnell.co/prospeaking/.


## Keep going

*Kristin Hayden shares...*
Kristin Hayden, "Everything Starts with Vision, Kristin Hayden, TEDxHimi," TED Video, October 3, 2017, http://www.youtube.com/watch?v=7iOk92jxZSk.

*Matt was body surfing...*
Tracy Seipel, "Remarkable recovery: Bay Area surfer who broke neck takes first steps," *The Mercury News*, December 22, 2017, http://www.mercurynews.com/2017/12/22/remarkable-recovery-bay-area-surfer-who-broke-neck-takes-first-steps/.

*Two people that day on the beach...*
Tracy Seipel, "Remarkable recovery: Bay Area surfer who broke neck takes first steps," *The Mercury News*, December 22, 2017, http://www.mercurynews.com/2017/12/22/remarkable-recovery-bay-area-surfer-who-broke-neck-takes-first-steps/.

# Gratitude

This book would not be possible without my speaker friends who inspired this project and shared their stories. To all of the Breakthrough Speakers featured in this book: thank you for being vulnerable, thank you for the work you do. Special thanks to everyone who gave their time to be interviewed: Cloe Shasha, Ashanti Branch, Dawn Fraser, Tiffany Yu, Shira Abramowitz, Monica Kang, Minda Harts, Antonio Neves, Tim Mousseau, James Robilotta, Amy Lazarus, Torin Perez, Nate Bagley, Avery Blank, Jenny Sauer-Klein.

To everyone who gifted their creative genius to make this book come to life: thank you. To my agent, Lindsay Edgecombe, and the entire team at Levine Greenberg Rostan: thank you for believing in this project and believing in me. Thank you to my editor Caroline Kessler and book designer Sumeet Banerji: working with you both for a second time was even more fun than *The Quarter-Life Breakthrough* round 1 in 2014! Thank you to my cover designer Samantha Russo: you're a brilliant artist. Thank you to the TarcherPerigee/Penguin Random House team that made my previous book possible (Jeanette Shaw, Amanda Shih, Lauren Appleton, Keely Platte, Zoe Norvell, Joel Fotinos, John Duff).

Thank you to my clients and everyone that has supported me in becoming a Breakthrough Speaker.

Special thanks to: the SpeakInc team (Rich Gibbons, Jeff Bigelow, Tim Mathy, Lisa Coleman, Nicole DeMers, Erin Lapeyre); Rhonda Payne, Karen Bernstein and everyone at ASAE; the CAMPUSPEAK team, David Stollman, Luke Davis, and Caitlin Smith; Hung Pham and Culture Summit; Jenny Sauer-Klein and The Culture Conference; Duleesha Kulasooriya and Deloitte; Robin Meyerhoff, Richard Green and SAP; Ashley Wilson and MailChimp; Cheryl Fraenzl, Dawn Fielding, Jennifer Jaffe and Esalen Institute; Ryan O'Rourke and AFLV; Markus von der Lühe and Year of the X; Jeremy Duhon, Jason Dilg, and TEDxMileHigh; Stacy Horne and The Battery; Sarah Shewey and EXP; Josh Linkler, Matt Ciccone, and 3 Ring Circus; Colette Crespin; everyone at Camp Grounded, Hive, REALITY Impact, and StartingBloc.

Thank you to the members and mentors of The Women Speaker Initiative, and everyone who is working to increase representation and opportunity in public speaking and across all industries. Special thanks to: Sarah K Peck, Lisa Lee, Nikita Mitchell, Danielle Bicknell, Dawn Fraser, Jess Ekstrom, Mia Birdsong, Antonio Neves, Tim Mousseau, James Robilotta, Vanessa Shaw, Jordan Axani, and Kunal Mehta.

Thank you to my beautiful friends who remind me what matters most, especially: Andreas Mendez-Peñate, Manuela Igel, Jesse Brenner, Gabe Prager, Kevin Haas, Zeb Zankel, Sarah Jesse, Brian Thomas, Phil Amidon, Brady Gil, Satya Kamdar, Kelly McFarling, Andy Saxon,

Dar Vanderbeck, Daniel Kahn, Sarah Fathallah, Jenny Feinberg, Christine Lai, Liz Beedy, EJ Winter, Ashley Hodge, Emma Sherwood-Forbes, Booth Haley, Iris Yee, Ryan Goldberg, Scott Goldberg, Zev Felix, Seth Felix, Brooke Dean, Bluma & Edward Felix, Kelsey Freeman, Emma Toll, Ashley Rose Hogrebe, Ilana Lipsett, Kiki Lipsett, Hana Nobel, Evan Gelfand, Terra Judge, Kelly Rogala, Jesse Rogala, Evan Kleiman, Jana Hirsch, Maribell Reyes, Ben Madden, Mordechai Weiner, Cam Adair, Nate Bagley, Ben Tseitlin, Alex McPhillips, Ivan Cash, Katrina Gordon, Lauren Burke, Emily Anhalt, Cosmo Fujiyama, Evan Walden, Cesar Gonzalez, Amber Rae, Farhad Attaie, Jessica Semaan, Janet Frishberg, Anna Akullian, Paloma Herman, Cassidy Blackwell, Morgan Davis, Minh Nguyen, Matt Lock, Saya Iwasaki, Earl Coleman, Erika Barraza, and Shelley Dyer. Levi Felix: I miss you brother. If we all could speak like you, this world would be a far brighter place.

Thank you to my family, Mom, Dad, Becca, Gemma, and Remy: I love you more than the world. Thank you to everyone that continues to carry me on my journey. You know who you are. I love you and I am forever grateful.

# About the Author

**ADAM SMILEY POSWOLSKY** is a millennial workplace expert, keynote speaker, and bestselling author of *The Quarter-Life Breakthrough* (TarcherPerigee/Penguin Random House).

Smiley helps companies attract, retain, and empower millennial talent, and he has inspired thousands of professionals to be more engaged at work, through speaking at companies like Unilever, IDEO, Salesforce, Genentech, Deloitte, SAP, Pinterest, and MailChimp. An internationally renowned motivational speaker, Smiley speaks about millennials, employee engagement, and intergenerational collaboration at Fortune 500 companies, business conferences, leadership trainings, and universities. His TEDx talk has been viewed over 450,000 times, and he has done hundreds of speaking engagements, reaching over 50,000 people in 10 countries.

Smiley's writing has been published in *The Washington Post*, *Fast Company*, *Quartz*, *Time*, and *Business Insider*, and his work has been featured in *USA Today*, *Inc.*, *Mashable*, *Forbes*, *VICE*, *CNN*, *CNBC*, *Cosmopolitan*, *MarketWatch* and the World Economic Forum, among others.

In 2017, Smiley launched The Women Speaker Initiative, a community that aims to increase the number of women and people of color speaking at conferences and companies, as well as ensure that underrepresented speakers are paid competitively as compared to their colleagues. The group now has over 1,000 members.

Smiley is a proud graduate of Wesleyan University, and can usually be found dancing in San Francisco, California (or in an airport en route to a speaking gig).

**Web:** smileyposwolsky.com
**Book:** thebreakthroughspeaker.com
**Instagram/Twitter:** @whatsupsmiley
**LinkedIn:** Adam Smiley Poswolsky

Smiley is available for speaking engagements as well as speaker trainings.

To inquire, please visit *smileyposwolsky.com/speaking*

Made in the USA
Monee, IL
31 January 2020